Grand-parenting REDEFINED

Guidance for Today's Changing Family

by Irene M. Endicott

Aglow Publications

A Ministry of Women's Aglow Fellowship, Int'l.
P.O. Box 1548
Lynnwood, WA 98046-1548
USA

Cover design by David Marty

Women's Aglow Fellowship, Int'l. is a non-denominational organization of Christian women. Our mission is to provide support, education, training and ministry opportunities to help women worldwide discover their true identity in Jesus Christ through the power of the Holy Spirit.

Aglow Publications is the publishing ministry of Women's Aglow Fellowship, Int'l. Our publications are used to help women find a personal relationship with Jesus Christ, to enhance growth in their Christian experience, and to help them recognize their roles and relationship according to scripture.

For more information about Women's Aglow Fellowship, please write to Women's Aglow Fellowship, Int'l., P.O. Box 1548, Lynnwood, WA 98046-1548, USA or call (206) 775-7282.

Unless otherwise noted, all scripture quotations in this publication are from the Holy Bible, New International Version. Copyright © 1973, 1978, 1984, International Bible Society. Other version abbreviated as follows: KJV (King James Version).

ISBN 0-932305-93-8

Dedicated to grandparents everywhere
who are trying to be all that
God wants them to be,

with special love to grandparents
experiencing more sorrow than joy.

You are not alone.

Acknowledgments

My deepest gratitude to each one who responded so graciously to my request for an original quote to precede the chapters in this book:

Ruth B. Graham, author and speaker; wife of world-renowned evangelist Billy Graham; one of America's best-known and best-loved grandmothers.

Florence Turnidge, Bible teacher, conference speaker, encourager, and grandmother; founder of "Helping Jesus Do His Work," a ministry to residents of nursing homes.

Beverly LaHaye, founder and president of Concerned Women For America; grandmother; author and nationally respected and admired advocate for women and families.

Colleen Townsend Evans, speaker, grandmother, and author of *A New Joy* and *Make Me Like You, Lord*; wife of Rev. Louis Evans.

Barbara Cook, pastor, counselor, retreat and conference speaker, grandmother; author of numerous books including *Ordinary Women—Extraordinary Strength* and *Love and Its Counterfeits*.

Michelle Cresse, national speaker on family issues; author of books including *Jigsaw Families, Solving the Puzzle of Remarriage*.

Gloria Gaither, best-selling author; award-winning songwriter and lyricist; gospel recording artist with her husband, Bill.

Helene Ashker, for more than thirty years, counselor and leader of women's ministries for The Navigators; author of *Jesus Cares For Women, A Leader's Guide For Hosting An Evangelistic Bible Study*.

Jean Lush, marriage and family therapist with CRISTA Counseling Service; grandmother; author of *Emotional Phases of a Woman's Life* and *Mothers and Sons*; popular

5

speaker at retreats and on national radio.

David Hocking, Bible teacher on Solid Rock Radio; senior pastor of Calvary Church of Santa Ana, California; grandfather.

Lillian Iverson, cofounder with her husband, Hegge, of Iverson Center, Christian counseling and adoption service; grandmother, speaker, and author of *Just Plain Vanilla*.

David Bragonier, director of Barnabus, Inc., a Christian financial teaching and training ministry; area coordinator for Larry Burkett's "Christian Financial Concepts."

Florence Littauer, prolific author of books for Christian women and families; president and founder of CLASS, Christian Leaders and Speakers Services; nationally-honored and in-demand speaker.

Paul LeBoutillier, Bible teacher, writer, Christian radio personality; senior pastor of Cornerstone Community Church, Ontario, Oregon.

Quin Sherrer, popular retreat and seminar speaker; grandmother; author of *How To Pray For Your Children* and coauthor of *How To Forgive Your Children*.

Edith Schaeffer, wife of the late Dr. Francis Schaeffer and author of numerous books, among them, *Everybody Can Know* and *L'Abri*, a book about the world-famous Christian community she founded.

Special thanks to:

Edith Schaeffer for permission to reprint her words from the famous book, *What Is A Family?*

Ruth B. Graham who handwrote her quote for this book, a document I will treasure and pass on to my daughter and granddaughter.

all of the courageous grandparents who shared their stories in the hope they might help someone else.

social service workers across the country who are doing the best job they can with limited resources and a lot of love.

experts from the fields of counseling, law, estate planning, and pastoring who offered valuable advice.

God bless each one of you for reaching out in this personal way to encourage grandparents in these changing times.

With love
to Christopher, Anna, Scott, Adam, Jeremy, Brian, Amy, Michelle, Samuel, Stewart, Olivia, and Gabrielle
. . . and their grandfather, my dear husband, Bill.

Contents

Foreword

You've heard the old saying, "There is nothing new under the sun." This book for active, involved, contemporary grandparents and their adult children soundly disproves that theory.

Grandparenting Redefined is the first book I've seen that deals with the radical changes in the grandparenting role and the difficult issues grandparents face today.

• Divorced children and grandchildren coming home to roost.

• Grandchildren who live far away.

• Grandparents giving up all they've worked for to raise a grandchild.

• Loaning money to grandchildren.

• Grandchildren who are far from God.

Grandparenting Redefined is a splendid training manual for grandparents, and I recommend reading it thoroughly before the job begins. Parenting skills alone are not enough for the grandparenting challenges ahead. In-depth training is needed in these changing times.

Hard issues and family secrets are exposed here. Irene Endicott examines them with intelligence and Christian compassion. Herself a grandmother of twelve, whose own mother was grandmother to twenty-eight and whose great-grandmother had one hundred-twenty-one direct descendants including thirty-seven grandchildren, Irene has watched grandparenting change over the years. She shares with us her own personal joys and sorrows as well as years of in-depth research and poignant conversations with grandparents from all over the country.

I believe God gave Irene a vision of the need for this book. It is loaded with hope and encouragement, grandparenting resources, Christian principles, and practical expert advice. Some of the stories will make you laugh; some will break your heart. You will be blessed by the messages from Ruth Graham, Gloria Gaither, Florence Littauer, and others—messages written especially for *Grandparenting Redefined*. You will cherish these gems of wisdom and spiritual truth, especially as you recognize the godly people who provided them.

A complete Christian guidebook for the contemporary grandparent of any age. Wonderfully new, tremendously needed.

Jean Lush

Introduction

Are you the grandparent of happy, healthy grandchildren living with both parents who are making ends meet financially and heading up a warm, loving Christ-centered home?

If you are, congratulations! Chances are that, in your circle of friends, is a grandparent who isn't and whose heart is breaking.

The stereotypical role my grandparents and probably yours lived out doesn't exist anymore. Today, as never before, grandparents are called upon for extraordinary service to their children and their children's children as young families wrestle with the enemies that wreck relationships, leaving precious grandchildren in the rubble.

• Five percent of America's families consist of a grandparent raising a grandchild.[1]

• Grandparents in forty-eight states express concern over lack of services and recognition of the plight of grandparents; grandparent support groups have sprung up all over the country.[2]

• One-third of initial child abuse calls received by children and youth agencies end with informal arrangements with relatives—mostly grandparents.[3]

Experts say thousands of other "informal arrangements" exist for one reason or another. Infants and children who suffer from their parents' dysfunctional lives usually have no one they (or the courts) can turn to but the grandparents. These little ones are innocent victims of:

• drug and alcohol abuse
• divorce
• stress
• physical, sexual, and/or emotional abuse
• abandonment

Families in emotional, spiritual, and financial bankruptcy can force today's grandparent into the unwanted role of mediator, money-lender and, yes, legal parent to their own grandchildren. Standing in the gap for young families, many of today's grandparents are making choices requiring sacrifice, risk, and incredible emotional and spiritual maturity. Choices like:

• whether or not to take on the responsibility of raising a grandchild.

• whether or not to take an adult child with kids back into their home when lives are crumbling.

• whether or not to loan money to children for the sake of grandchildren.

This book looks at the changes in grandparenting in America. It chronicles true stories of grandparents facing difficult relational issues in these changing times and basing hard choices on a foundation of the Word of God and finding it faithful. Some names and circumstances have been changed as a protection.

I hope you are experiencing grandparenting as God intended it and as you always thought it would be. But if you aren't, you are not alone. Just as surely as God knows the depth of your love, he knows, too, your anguish when faint cracks appear in relationships and when those small fractures become deep, dark crevices that seem beyond repair.

God is faithful. His Word prepares us to face troubled times and sustains us in the valleys. He can repair the damage and replace the loss with gain.

Grandparenting has changed. It will never be the same again. Grandparents are different, too. But God does not change. He is the same yesterday, today, and tomorrow—the only one in whom we can place our trust.

Be encouraged. All things work together for good to those who love the Lord. By the power of the Holy Spirit and the infinite love and mercy of Jesus Christ, grandparents' lives *can* be forever changed to the glory of God, the Father.

My hope is that, as you read this book, one of those lives will be *yours*.

Our children were blessed with the best of grandparents. They were fun and played games with the children. They tolerated no disrespect or disobedience and told stories of their twenty-five years as medical missionaries in China.

Mother loved to do handwork, sewing doll clothes for the girls. She made great fudge; scraping the fudge pan was the best part.

Thanksgiving, Christmas, and Sunday dinners were shared events at their home or ours. A combination of love, practical godliness, and fun made them grandparents we feel were God's special gift to our children.

If your grandparenting season is not like this, remember Jesus Christ knows. Place your trust in him.

Ruth B. Graham

1
...
What Is
a Grandparent?

JOB DESCRIPTION

Place of Employment: Anywhere
Hours: Anytime
Qualifications: The love of Jesus Christ, the patience of Job, the wisdom of Solomon, the grace of God, the forgiveness of the Holy Spirit, the perseverance of Paul, and a sense of humor.
Salary: Heavenly. To be negotiated.

How does that job description match up with your grandparenting season? If it fits, you are experiencing grandparenting without trauma. Without the disappointment of breaking or damaged relationships. Grandparenting as God intended it to be.

Perhaps, though, the words grace, forgiveness, and

perseverance struck an ominous chord deep in your heart because some of your grandparenting experiences can best be described as a patchwork of relationships and responsibilities. Perhaps you have fallen for the world's expectations. You appear lighthearted when you don't feel lighthearted. You speak glowingly to your friends about the grandchildren, leaving out the negatives, the gory details of pending divorce or other serious circumstances. You're not alone. You're not the only one trying to live up to Erma Bombeck-style of grandparenting and suffering in silence.

ERMA'S JOB DESCRIPTION

• A grandparent can always be counted upon to buy anything you're selling, from all-purpose greeting cards to peanut brittle, from flower seeds to cookies, from transparent tape to ten chances on a pony.

• A grandparent buys you gifts your mother says you don't need.

• A grandparent will put a sweater on you when she is cold, feed you when she is hungry, and put you to bed when she is tired.

• A grandparent is the only baby-sitter who doesn't charge money to keep you.[1]

Such simple, lighthearted truths can become heavy expectations. Grandparenting is not that easy. For example, you'll find that many of today's grandparents are the ones supplying a grandchild's basic needs. These grandparents are the *only* caregivers of the grandchild because the parents are either absent or incapable of giving.

YOUR OWN JOB DESCRIPTION

How are you doing? Try writing a job description for grandparenting as you are experiencing it. Then honestly evaluate your progress toward becoming a healthy role model. Following is a sample of what you might come up with:

I have	Yes	No	Working On It
the love of Jesus Christ	❑	❑	❑
the patience of Job	❑	❑	❑
the wisdom of Solomon	❑	❑	❑
the forgiveness of the Holy Spirit	❑	❑	❑
the perseverance of Paul	❑	❑	❑
a sense of humor	❑	❑	❑

I am expected to		
be available at any time	❑	❑
work for nothing	❑	❑
lead rather than follow	❑	❑
follow rather than lead	❑	❑

I like my job just as it is because: _____

_____

_____

I would change my job by: _____

_____

_____

My grandparenting goal is: _____

_____

_____

What are you giving? What are you receiving? What are *your* expectations as a grandparent in your unique circumstances? As you evaluate your true reality in this season of your life, you can determine what, if anything, you can do to achieve your grandparenting goals.

SETTING GRANDPARENTING GOALS

Some grandparents are "labeled" and aren't ever aware of it:

• The "dutiful grandparent" everyone can count on.

• The "crafty grandparent" whose artistic gifts are used for the benefit of the family.

• The "quiet grandparent" who waits until asked.

• The "take-charge grandparent" found in leadership roles in family activities or celebrations.

• The "wise grandparent" the children seek out for answers.

• The "spiritual grandparent" the whole family looks to for nurturing and guidance in the Christian walk.

Your label may be a combination of two or more of these and other qualities. Of course, all of these labels are positive. Aren't they?

Does your label fit your idea of the grandparent you are or want to be? I have found that setting goals, even in personal relationships, helps me keep my life on track. Time goes by so quickly. Children grow up so fast!

It is beneficial to evaluate yours and other's views of yourself in order to fulfill your special role of "grandparent."

DOES ANYBODY CARE?

In 1990, the U.S. Bureau of Census asked the person filling out the questionnaire what his/her relationship to the others living in that home was. No doubt many were grandparents. But millions of grandparents in our country go uncounted.

The American Association of Retired Persons (AARP), a powerful national lobbying organization for older people, doesn't know the number of grandparents. They know about medical needs, political desires, and buying habits of older persons and offer some tremendous services for retirees. But the title "Grandparent" is a tough one to get a handle on in America.

Maybe the reason we are not specifically "tracked" like other population groups is that we don't fit into a category. We range in age from mid-thirties to over one hundred. Since many of us travel and enjoy the golden years of retirement, we could be considered "transient." *Not a complimentary thought.*

There is one place where the number of grandparents is recorded. A place where the name, address, phone number, likes, dislikes, numbers of grandchildren, and everything about those grandchildren, even to the number of hairs on their heads, is written down for eternity. It is the Book of Life, where every detail is inscribed until the Day of Judgment. The Writer is our Lord and Savior, Jesus Christ, the Keeper of the only records that count, and the One who knows every grandparent's innermost thoughts. He rejoices in our joy and he alone can mend the cracks.

It doesn't matter that we don't seem important enough to be entered into the books of the world. What matters is that Almighty God knows everything. He cares about every single one of us! "See, I have engraved you on the palms of my hands" (Isa. 49:16).

ACCEPTING THE JOB

Most of us look forward to becoming grandparents. Some call it our "reward." Others, a "privilege of age."

Grandparenting Redefined

Many of us, though, ran to the mirror and checked for wrinkles when we got the word. A tiny voice from deep within whispered, "They can't be talking about *me*!"

That's how it was for me. Frankly, at thirty-six years old, I wasn't thinking about it.

Bill and I are in a second marriage of twenty-four years, and his three kids gave him grandchildren before my four did. I wasn't thinking about the fact that someday those babes would bounce through my door and call me "Grandma." Horrors!

When it finally happened, I didn't have a chance against three-and-a-half-year-old Adam.

Bill, Jr., and his family had done their lonely stint in the Navy at Reykjavik, Iceland and wrote that they would soon arrive to live in Washington. Grandpa, of course, was ecstatic that now Adam and six-year-old Anna would grow up before his very eyes. Grandparent heaven! *Imagine a grown man jumping around like that!*

On the day of their arrival, friends were visiting, and I was upstairs adding a few last-minute items to a rummage sale box. Like the brown and black spotted nightgown I had worn for ten years. How could I bear to part with it? After all, I wore that *before* I was a grandparent.

As I tossed it on top of the box, the doorbell rang. I dashed downstairs in time to see Grandpa open the front door. It was the kids! I had seen pictures but had not met the children.

"Why, they're the most beautiful grandchildren in the whole world!" I felt the wall of resistance around my heart crumble. I was a stepgrandma to these two perfect little people? *Imagine a grown woman jumping around like that!*

Anna, the shy, demure one, hid behind Grampa's leg as our friends greeted her. But where was Adam? He was there a second ago!

24

Friends and family scoured the house. "Adam! Adam! Where are you?" Not a sign downstairs.

The searchers assembled in the living room, their faces beginning to show signs of worry when we heard a "clump, clump" sound.

All heads turned toward the stairway. Coming down the steps were the toes of two size-four sneakers peeking out from under the hem of my nightgown with the brown and black spots. Adam's tiny hands were stretched high, holding the straps and his pug nose indented the soft, silky material. He stopped in the middle of the stairway. "Is this your lion suit, Grandma?" he mumbled through the fabric.

My face no doubt turned every shade of red in the rainbow. Grandpa is still laughing today.

Now, twelve years later, I remember that entrance as more prophetic than funny. That was the time when midlife became the rummage of precious memories and my "lion suit" was replaced by the whole armor of God for the season of life that lay ahead. I had stuffed the fact that I was a grandma and now Adam had laid it out for all the world to see.

By the time one of "my own" gave me a grandchild, the Lord had sufficiently humbled me to receive *all* of them as mine. But it wasn't easy.

• I was mistaken for the mother at school carnivals.

• I felt the sting of the arrow piercing my ego when Bill began calling me "Grandma" instead of "Dear" or "Honey" or "Irene" as he had "before."

• I found those first gray hairs and have irrefutable evidence that they are a direct result of grandparenting.

I figured I'd better face up to it and learn everything I could about this job in order to function well in my role. I accepted the fact that grandparenting is the will of my Sovereign God for me at this time of my life, and I have

25

much to learn. Some of the greatest lessons still lie ahead, and I am privileged to be called "Grandma."

HOW DO WE DO IT?

Like motherhood, this job is a mystery until we live it. There is no Grandparenting University. So how do we do it? And whose expectations of us really matter? Ours? The world's? God's?

It is in the Word that we find the expectations for grandparenting; if adhered to, we can live in triumph over any and all circumstances.

Our Father asks that we believe on the risen Lord Jesus Christ and that we tell others about him. How happy it must make him when his older children bring the little ones to him.

With marching orders from God's holy word, grandparents are soldiers of salvation by prayer, thought, and deed.

Keeping active for the Lord brings great fulfillment, and when the children are part of it, the blessings multiply beyond expectation.

For a God who loves us so much and expects so little, can we do any less than bring his children closer to him?

Florence Turnidge

2

...

God's Expectations

Although Scripture offers little in the way of a job description for grandparents, certain verses define what God had in mind when he created the position.

"Children's children are a crown to the aged, and parents are the pride of their children" (Prov. 17:6) is his indication of mutual reward in this job. More than that, it is his expectation for the conduct of all parties.

Do you think of your grandchildren as your crown? They are. An awesome gift from God. However, no royalty ever wears a crown without acknowledging the responsibility that goes with it. So it is for us.

BE AN EXAMPLE

Grandchildren learn by our example just what it is that God expects from his children. "These are the commands, decrees and laws the Lord your God directed me to teach you to observe in the land you are crossing the Jordan to possess, so that you, your children and their children after them may fear the Lord your God as long as you live by keeping all his decrees and commands that I give you, and so that you may enjoy long life" (Deut. 6:1-2).

Florence Turnidge, longtime Bible teacher and encourager, has a new ministry in her seventieth year — visiting residents of nursing homes with her grandchildren. Four-year-old Jordan calls it "helping Jesus do his work." Indeed, the welcome visits from Florence and her bright, loving little ones bring hugs, songs, and prayers to older people. And the kids observe firsthand the love of Jesus Christ through Grandma Turnidge.

Florence says, "All children have in them the potential for ministry. Youth is no barrier. In fact, when a preschooler puts his or her arms around a centenarian, age melts away. Old faces become young again and beam with love as they join the children in a chorus of 'Jesus loves all the grandmas and grandpas of the world!'"[1]

What Florence and her two-and-a-half-year-old granddaughter, Jennifer, began in one nursing home five years ago has grown to many other sites throughout Seattle, involving mothers and grandmothers, young and old, and their children.

In Genesis 48, a father honored his father who was ill. Joseph visited Israel (Jacob), perhaps in a nursing home, taking along his two sons, Manasseh and Ephraim. We read in verse two that when Israel was told they had come, he "rallied his strength and sat up on the bed."

When Israel saw the sons of Joseph, he asked, "Who are these?"

"They are the sons God has given me here," Joseph said to his father.

Then Israel said, "Bring them to me so I may bless them."

Now Israel's eyes were failing because of old age, and he could hardly see. So Joseph brought his sons close to him, and his father kissed them and embraced them.

Israel said to Joseph, "I never expected to see your face again, and now God has allowed me to see your children too."

Then Joseph removed them from Israel's knees and bowed down with his face to the ground. And Joseph took both of them, Ephraim on his right . . . and Manasseh on his left . . . and brought them close to him. . .

Then Israel blessed Joseph and said,

"May the God before whom my fathers Abraham and Isaac walked, the God who has been my shepherd all my life to this day, the Angel who has delivered me from all harm—may he bless these boys. May they be called by my name and the names of my fathers Abraham and Isaac, and may they increase greatly upon the earth" (Gen. 48:8-13, 15).

Grandfather Jacob conferred God's blessing upon his grandsons that they might be committed to the Lord, strengthened by God's grace, and guided by God's will. This kind of Christ-like example to children will stay with them all of their lives.

BE A WITNESS

Edith Schaeffer, wife of the late Dr. Francis Schaeffer, founder of L'Abri, the world-renowned Christian community in Switzerland, states the case for Christian witness to our children so clearly: "The truth of the existence and the character of God is to be made known to the children and the children's children. We are responsible for our children and for our grandchildren, for our nieces and nephews and our grandnieces and grandnephews. That they may know what? The wonder of who God is, what God has done, what God has said, and what He has meant to those doing the telling."[2]

God clearly exhorted Moses in the book of Exodus to pass along a legacy to his grandchildren by telling about all that the Lord had done for him and others.

"Then the Lord said to Moses, 'Go to Pharaoh, for I have hardened his heart and the hearts of his officials so that I may perform these miraculous signs of mine among them that you may tell your children and grandchildren how I dealt harshly with the Egyptians and how I performed my signs among them and that they may know that I am the Lord" (Ex. 10:1, 2).

And in Deuteronomy we read, "Only be careful, and watch yourselves closely so that you do not forget the things your eyes have seen or let them slip from your heart as long as you live. Teach them to your children and to their children after them" (Deut. 4:9).

As Florence, Jacob, and Joseph have witnessed by their example to children, the flood of love and caring spills over to all of us. That's what God wants us to do; let his love flow through for all to see, hear, and have. The Holy Spirit can use each of us as a catalyst to bring new life— eternal life—to others! Ask God what it is he wants *you* to do. How can you show his love to your grandchildren? How can he move among the people through you?

FIND THE JOY

"May the Lord bless you from Zion all the days of your life; may you see the prosperity of Jerusalem and may you live to see your children's children" (Ps. 128:5-6) is God's poignant expression of hope for us as grandparents. He asks that we sift and sort the circumstances of our grandchildren's lives, find the joy of this season, and dwell on it.

It is difficult to find the joy in some of the circumstances of our children's lives today. Yet millions of young families in America are walking closely with the Lord, raising godly kids who prayerfully will be the leaders of tomorrow. Rejoice in that knowledge and in the knowledge that our God is the restorer of joy.

One day, during my quiet time with the Lord, he revealed hidden joy to me. Our son had announced a pending divorce, the consequences of which would fall on the small shoulders of two of our grandchildren. Another family split in two.

I pleaded with God for relief. I poured out my heart to the God of all mercy and understanding. In the quiet darkness, my thoughts drifted back through the years to my son's boyhood. I thought about how much his son today looks like him. I pictured my granddaughter's sweet face. Wonderful memories of the last eight years flashed before me, memories I would not have if this marriage had not taken place. I was smiling!

I could not control that marriage. I had to *find* the joy in it. God taught me to pluck out the good and cling to it, to build on it for the future. I concentrated on being a stabilizing influence on my grandchildren's lives. I can honestly say today, two years later, that our son and his ex-wife have done an outstanding job of parenting and, with counseling and prayer, we all have a measure of peace and hope for the future.

The builder Nehemiah said, "This day is sacred to our Lord. Do not grieve, for the joy of the Lord is your strength" (Neh. 8:10). Praise him for joy!

OUR ACTIONS AFFECT OTHERS

Here is a sobering word for those of us who are not yet grandparents from pastor and Bible teacher, Paul LeBoutillier:

Scripture tells us the great effect a grandparent can have on his or her family *before* they became a grandparent. Particularly in the Old Testament, the seeds of one's younger life are depicted as 'blooming' in later generations either in a positive or negative manner. The Apostle Paul makes a remark about Timothy's mother and grandmother as having had a positive (godly) effect on the young man Timothy (2 Timothy 1:5). The passage doesn't tell us if Timothy actually ever knew his grandmother, only that she was a godly woman and that she passed her faith on to her daughter (Eunice) who of course was Timothy's mother. In this way, grandparents are seen as providing a rich heritage of godliness.

The emphasis, however, lies in the kind of life they lived *before* they became grandparents, while not taking anything away from the continued positive influence they can be to their children and grandchildren in later years. (See also Psalm 103:17 and Jeremiah 2:9.)[3]

God is concerned that he communicate to his people the tremendous importance and consequence of their actions. He would remind them that their own actions affect others for generations.

This then is what God expects of grandparents:
• Be an example.
• Be a witness.

• Find the joy.

• Remember that our actions affect others for generations.

A clear job description that we as grandparents must take seriously.

We live in changing times. Some changes are for good and some are upsetting and disconcerting. The family has changed. Grandparenting has changed.

But all changes must be measured by an authority that is unchanging and constant. This is necessary to make sure we are not conforming to a world that will lead us into harmful changes.

Our absolute measure must be the Word of God. As Hebrews 13:8 reminds us, Jesus Christ is the same yesterday and today and forever.

Beverly LaHaye

3
...
Yesterday and Today

Grandparents Henrietta and David Karber were honored on the cover of the March, 1990 issue of *Focus on the Family*. The Karbers left Eastern Europe for America in the 1870s and settled in Oklahoma. With the help of other Mennonite immigrants, they built a new church and called it Hoffnungsfeld—Field of Hope. Grandma and Grandpa Karber chose to invest in eternal things. They chose to honor God above all else and passed that legacy on to the generations that followed and specifically, to their great-granddaughter, Caralee.

Following are some of this granddaughter's dearest recollections of her grandparents. You might recognize one or two:

- sweet peas and roses in the garden by the front door
- the aroma of freshly baked bread
- crisp fried chicken

- stick-to-your-ribs hot oatmeal
- rubbing alcohol, Mentholatum, and warm flannel rags
- Chamberlain's Stomach Potient
- Sweetheart soap and water
- coloring Easter eggs
- hugs
- pretend church services on the porch
- huddling by the heat register as Grandpa read the Bible
- praying together

Caralee says, "Grandma and Grandpa started each day with God's Word because it had been their sure foundation in the past and it would be their guiding light for the future. Their final possessions were few, yet they died wealthy. As son and daughter of the King, they owned a storehouse of accomplishments and memories. It's doubtful any book will be written about them. No monuments will be erected in their honor. But all three of our sons have made a commitment to Jesus Christ and are a part of the living memorial to Grandma and Grandpa's greatest accomplishment—influencing others for Christ."[1]

YESTERDAY

I hope you have pleasant memories of your grandparents. I've always felt sad for my husband because he grew up without grandparents. I can hardly imagine that since I was privileged to have such an excellent model in my growing up years. My mother's mother, Grandma Burch, pioneered in the Old West of the late 1800s. She was sturdy stock. A survivor.

Grandparents are strong.

Grandma was one of few women in the territory skilled at nursing and served as midwife for many births in the fledgling town of Deer Lodge, Montana at the turn of the century.

Grandparents are smart.

She and Grandpa made their own contributions to the town's growth, giving birth to my mother and her sixteen siblings who in turn presented Grandma and Grandpa with thirty-seven grandchildren and ten great-grandchildren.

Grandparents are healthy.

Grandpa taught all eight of his sons how to ride a horse and how to grow anything in Montana earth that was hard and unrelenting one season and soft and giving the next. And he taught them right from wrong without using a whip.

Grandma taught her nine daughters how to sew, cook, and make roses, carnations, and mums out of painted paper and wire—flowers that looked like the real thing. The girls sold them on the street corners of downtown Deer Lodge for money to help support their large family and to buy a Christmas present for their parents.

Grandparents are skilled.

Grandma told fascinating stories about Indians, surviving the elements, and man's inhumanity to man as experienced by a young girl in an uncharted land. I especially loved the funny stories about lay-preachers who "moseyed onto the property" to see Grandpa.

One such tale, told by Grandma, has survived four generations. It's the gripping saga of the visiting preacher at the front door of the log house and the renegade Indian sneaking in the back. As the story goes, Grandma opened the door to greet the preacher. He spotted the intruder behind her, and rushing to pick up the hand-fashioned fireplace iron, raised it high above his head to deliver the saving blow that would render the man harmless.

When his shiny black suit pants suddenly fell to his ankles.

One more step and feet met fabric, causing him to

sprawl head-over-teakettle across the floor. Quick-thinking Grandma spotted the Indian, picked up a hot pot from the wood stove, and scalded the invader, who hightailed it out the backdoor, never to be seen again.

I don't know whether this well-worn tale contains a grain of truth.

Grandparents are storytellers.

Grandma always found a way to make us laugh, even when she didn't know we were watching. At the end of a busy day, she'd sit in her handmade rocking chair by the old wood stove, gently place her "newfangled" teeth on the table, and gum some peanuts in the shell. She'd rock and chew. Rock and chew. Back and forth. Sometimes fast. Sometimes slow. To a rhythm only she could hear.

Grandparents are funny.

Grandma had the right answer for every question. She never yelled at me when I made an awful racket, jumping up and down on the tin roof of her root cellar where she kept all those wonderful homemade jams, pickles, and fresh-picked vegetables and fruits. Or when I woke everyone up in the middle of the night to go to the outhouse. Grandma allowed me to have coffee loaded with fresh cream and heaps of sugar when I was nine years old and Mother said I couldn't.

I remember watching in childlike wonder as Grandma Burch loosed the tattered old cloth clip from the back of her head, sending her shimmering silver hair all the way to the floor. I thought then that Grandma was the most beautiful lady I had ever seen. I still do.

Grandparents are wise, patient, kind, and beautiful.

We revered and adored my grandparents and considered it a privilege to visit their home. They had a certain invisible and irrevocable license to do and say anything because, in our eyes, they could do no wrong.

I'm the third youngest child of eleven born in Pocatello, Idaho, and I can tell you my mother learned her lessons well. She died in 1982, grandparent of twenty-eight and great-grandmother of seven.

The jewels in my dear mother's crown are beyond number and brilliance. Each of the eleven of us were born two years apart. Dad worked in foreign countries as a construction comptroller on two-year contracts, missing most of our births and most of our graduations. Two of my siblings died in infancy from diseases easily treated today. Mom raised the surviving nine of us through the Depression, World War II, measles, chicken pox, and mumps—alone.

The same reverence accorded her parents was well-earned by my mother.

CHANGING TIMES

Over the years of my mother's grandparenting season, after World War II, things began to change. Her children and their children landed on her doorstep, sometimes in the middle of the night, sometimes running from the law. She always welcomed and sheltered them. Children of divorce took up residence with her. She cooked and cleaned for them and sent them on their way to the next battle. A child calling from another state in need of money always got it. Parts of breaking families ended up on her kitchen floor, each with their own tale of woe. In 1965, one of those families was mine. She always listened. She always tried to help. At what cost? That question goes unanswered.

Wait a minute! Grandparents are strong, smart, healthy, skilled, funny, wise, patient, kind, and beautiful. Where is the reward for such excellence and boundless sacrifice?

TODAY

I have no doubt that today's grandparents have the same wonderful qualities as those of previous generations. I strive for those traits and pray for them daily. I'm sure you do, too. However, because of the fast pace and the pressures of the day in which we live, some new adjectives describe today's grandparents.

Busy. Working. Stressed.

It may be necessary today for one or both grandparents to work at full- or part-time jobs to realize their dreams for a secure future. That leaves less time available for the grandkids.

And you won't often find Granny in a rocking chair, either. More than likely, she's involved in a career, working out at the health club, volunteering for a good cause, shopping at the mall, and/or traveling the world!

Grandparents have also experienced some attitude changes—dealing with how they view themselves and how others view them. Today's great-grandparents survived the Depression and the thirties, and they suffered the deaths of many of their grandchildren in World War II. Survival and suffering were the order of the day.

After World War II and in the fifties, grandparents who had taken the place of soldier sons and daughters in America's factories and shipyards stayed in the work force. This was the beginning of the changing face of grandparenting as we knew it. Through the turbulent sixties and seventies, as the cost of living and essentials like medical care soared, grandparents brought their own agendas into the eighties and nineties.

Still, no matter what changes around us, no matter what generation we find ourselves grandparenting, one thing remains constant: our abiding love for our grandchildren.

I think that's why God made grandparents. So that the little ones he loves so much can see the consistency of his love mirrored in our lives.

Now, as baby boomers begin to trade such labels as "Young Upwardly Mobile Professional" for the title of "Grandparent," won't it be interesting to watch how they approach this important job? Will they have a survival-and-suffering-mentality like their grandparents and great-grandparents? I doubt it. How will the restless discontent of the Vietnam War era and the "Me" generation affect their grandparenting styles and attitudes? What influence will their life-experiences have on grandchildren of tomorrow?

Maybe you're like me. I raised my kids through the emergence of the national drug tragedy in the sixties and seventies. We got through it by God's grace, and I am proud of my adult children. Through their growing up years, I watched the divorce rate rise and the crime rate increase and had no thought those statistics would touch my life.

Today, my seven children and stepchildren have given me twelve grandchildren of my own, and I have tasted some bitter fruit. Now I know, just as you probably do, that the job description for grandparenting has changed. I'm not sure yet whether it is the circumstances of young families or the attitudes of grandparents that have changed the most. Maybe it's fifty-fifty. I do know that stark statistics tell the stories of mothers, fathers, and their children tangled in webs of divorce, abuse, and abandonment.

• If the current trend continues, one out of every two marriages that have occurred since the early seventies will end in divorce.[2]

• In 1990, 2.5 million American children were reported abused, usually in the home and usually by someone the child knew.[3]

- One-half of the children raised by substance-abusing parents will become addicts themselves.[4]

But somebody is missing from these statistics! What about the grandparents?

We mourn the losses. Our hearts ache. And we are the ones who pick up the pieces of millions of American children's shattered lives today.

Researching this book, I was surprised by the enthusiasm of grandparents to tell their stories—to vent bottled-up feelings and emotions that have spilled out with puddles of tears, sometimes for hours at a time. I learned that I was not alone.

God has also affirmed me that, even though he has allowed the changes and the deep valleys in our grandparenting lives, he was and is faithful to his promises.

"Praise be to the God and Father of our Lord Jesus Christ, the Father of compassion and the God of all comfort, who comforts us in all our troubles, so that we can comfort those in any trouble. . . . For just as the sufferings of Christ flow over into our lives, so also through Christ our comfort overflows" (2 Cor. 1:3-5).

Loving God . . .
I know my grandchildren need my time,
They deserve my time,
So, while they still want my time,
Help me to make the time,
While I still have the time.

Holy God . . . .
Keep me faithful
To use the time entrusted to me
Wisely, creatively, unselfishly,
In the lives of those I love.
                    Amen

                    Colleen Townsend Evans

4
···

Mountain Time/ Standard Time

Some people long for yesterday's "simplicity." Do you? As a grandmother, I don't. Along with all of the pleasant memories, I have early recollections of my Grandma Burch out on the back porch, laboring over the washboard until her knuckles showed red and the veins on the back of her hands stood out from the strain of hand-wringing and hanging up clothes for as many as seventeen children. She used crude implements to accomplish tasks, both the routine and difficult. As a grandparent, my mother used a hand-wringer model to wash clothes and was thrilled to have it. Dryers came along after we children were raised. Every area of life was more complicated than today, including transportation and medical care.

What is it that remains the same yesterday and today? Time. There has always been time to spend with those we love. But it's never enough! Today, in our faster-paced world, we have to *make* time to do the things we want to do, and we have to make conscious choices about what those things are.

I submit that, in the golden years of life, we will find eternal value in choosing to spend time with our grandchildren.

There are two kinds of grandparenting time.

MOUNTAIN TIME

Dr. Martin Luther King, in his last speech before his death, said, "I have been to the mountaintop. God has allowed me to go up to the mountain and I have looked over."[1]

He had been to the highest place where God acknowledged all of his work, all of his sacrifice, and all of his faith. Dr. King did not say, "I have taken myself to the mountaintop by all of my good works." He did not say, "I have been to the mountaintop because I deserve it." God took him there, to the highest place and allowed him to "look over."

That's Mountain Time, the highest quality time. And we can have it with our grandchildren. To achieve it, though, we must allow God to work through us.

STANDARD TIME

Standard Time is doing what we have to do, getting by as a grandparent. Enjoying the grandchildren when we see them. Doing our duty because we happen to have the job.

If you are on Standard Time with your grandchildren, you are missing some of the greatest blessings of your grandparenting life.

Strive for the mountaintop.

TAKING TIME

What does spending quality time with your grandchildren mean to you? Is it taking them to a special place? On a long trip? Is it spending quiet hours together, talking and listening? Do you have to plan this time or can it happen spontaneously as only the Lord can plan it?

Whatever form it takes, make opportunities to teach the children something or to learn something together. The smallest or seemingly insignificant times with your grandchildren might be the most memorable to them as they grow older.

Sometimes we need a "swift kick," as Grandma Burch used to say, to realize just how blessed we are to have any time at all with our grandchildren. Six-year-old Jeremy pointed me to the mountain.

"Faster than a speeding bullet! Able to leap tall buildings in a single bound! Superman!"

Those sounds from the family room meant Jeremy was visiting. It was Sunday afternoon and I had promised to babysit Jeremy and his little sister, Amy.

"Soomerman" was what he called the video when he was Amy's age. Now, at six, he could tell us exactly what was going to happen moment by moment, and when we needed to fast-forward "to get through the boring parts."

My previous week's daily routine had suffered interruption after interruption, and I planned to use Sunday to catch up. I figured as soon as the kids arrived, Jeremy would want to see "Superman" and sweet little Amy never gets far away from her brother, so, like a good grandma, I could plunk them in front of the TV and get about my important work around the house.

I forgot that Jeremy doesn't like to watch the "scary parts" without an adult present. Five minutes into the

51

movie, he called to me in the kitchen, "Grandma! Please come sit with me. I'm scared of this part! Please?"

I dried my hands, put the broom away, and left my important work to sit with Jeremy and Amy at the TV.

The scary part over, I returned to the kitchen when, after about five minutes, Jeremy called, "Grandma! Please come back and sit with me. I'm scared of this part! Please?"

Back I went. Several times. I got so I could tell when it was time to fast-forward through the boring parts. Each time, I edged back to the kitchen when, you guessed it . . .

"Grandma! Please come sit with me. I'm scared of this part! Please?"

I gave up. Might as well sit through the whole video and be near the children. I wouldn't get anything done this afternoon.

Resigned, I walked back into the family room and noticed how the sun from the window danced on Amy's blond ponytail. She held her arms up to me. Her sweet little face radiated love and, for that moment, Grandma was the only person in her world.

What a responsibility!

"Thank you, Grandma," she purred against my neck. Amy sat on my lap behind Jeremy, who was sprawled on the floor in front of the television set, totally engrossed in "Superman," or so I thought.

The bad guys took away the kryptonite and rendered Superman weak, all of his power gone. I didn't even blink so as not to miss a scene during this exciting part of the movie.

In the middle of the excitement, Jeremy stood up, turned around, put his arms around me and gave me a big, warm hug.

Startled, I whispered against his shoulder, "What is this for?"

"Oh, I was just sitting there thinking how lucky I am to have a grandma like you who sits with me during the scary parts. I love you, Grandma."

Three-year-old Amy joined in the hug. "I love you, too, Grandma."

For a long, unforgettable moment, the three of us clung together there on the sofa.

While Superman was overpowered by the bad guys.

While the important kitchen work waited.

While Grandma Endicott moved from Standard Time to Mountain Time.

The song says, "You may be the only Jesus some will ever see." You may be that person in your grandchild's life who can give that quality time, that love, that life-changing care.

Don't miss the opportunity.

It won't work out right every time, though. Try as you might, you're bound to goof once in a while. For example, you might have a grandchild who is preschool age and you catch yourself treating her or him like a baby. Grandpa Endicott will tell you that doesn't work. And it's downright embarrassing to be brought up short by a little guy like Adam.

LETTING THEM GROW

Adam reached what his Grandpa calls the "Why Age." Why not? Why did you do that? Why can't I have it? Why can't I go? Why? My husband had built a small workbench beside his big one so Adam could work "alongside" his grandpa with small tools. On a hot summer day, both pounded away at the bench, Grandpa building a cabinet and Adam working on his one-of-a-kind wooden hydroplane.

"Adam, what are you going to be when you grow up?" Grandpa watched carefully to see where his big hammer hit.

Grandparenting Redefined

Without breaking the sequence of hits with his hammer, Adam replied casually, "Oh, a lawyer or president."

"Whoa," said Grandpa, continuing his work. "President of the United States?"

"Yup. Why?"

"Oh, boy! If you become president of the United States and Grandpa comes to visit you, a secretary will come out and say to me, 'I'm sorry, sir, but the President is busy.'"

"Yup. Why?"

"And I'll say, 'But I'm his grandpa! He'll see me!' And the secretary will say, 'Sit over there.'"

"Yup. Why?"

"And Grandpa will sit there and sit there for hours and hours and another secretary will come out and say, 'I'm sorry, sir, but the president can't see you today and . . .'"

"Yup. Why?"

"And I'll say, 'But you can't do that. I'm his grandpa! You just go in there and tell him . . .'"

Without looking up, continuing to hammer, Adam interrupted his grandfather, saying, "Why do you care, Grandpa? You'll be dead then anyway!"

Wise beyond his years, maybe Adam *will* become President.

Grandpa, accustomed to treating our grandson like a baby, finally recognized that Adam was growing up. Thus began a new relationship between Grandpa and his bright and inquisitive grandson. Grandpa learned that Mountain Time includes being flexible to change with the child.

"Talking down" to grandchildren is an easy trap to fall into. It's our way of keeping them little. I know a grandmother who stood in front of the hospital nursery window, crying uncontrollably as she looked longingly at her just-born grandson sleeping peacefully on the other side of the glass. Her sad tears attracted a small crowd and someone asked what was wrong. She responded, "It's just that someday he's going to grow up!"

Daughters and daughters-in-law usually watch the silly talking pretty closely. For example, if a child can only say "airpanes" and "airpote," some well-meaning grandmas will repeat the words as the child says them and get caught at it. Of course, I was never found guilty of such a thing, you understand! Little children learn from correct pronunciation and honest speech.

Speaking to him on his level became an important issue to Adam at around age six or seven. Even today, at age sixteen, Adam tests the veracity of any given thing. One day, I was talking with his sister, Anna, about my upcoming fifty-fifth birthday when Adam walked into the room.

"I'm going to be the speed limit next month, Adam," I said.

He tossed me one of those grins that make me want to run for cover and said, "Speed limit, Grandma? In which state?"

SHARING THE WORD

You probably have favorite ways to share the Word with your grandchildren. Does a greater joy exist than knowing that they are absorbing, understanding, yes, even hungering for God's Word? What a privilege it is to have a role in that life-giving process!

Grandpa Endicott has a special game he plays with Chris, Brian, and Scott, our grandchildren who live in Fresno, California. Their bedroom walls are decorated with awards for Bible memorization. When Grandpa visits, they run for their Bibles for Grandpa's Bible Drill.

With Bibles in hand and sitting cross-legged on the floor, the boys eagerly look up to Grandpa, who thoroughly enjoys the moment. Grandpa ponders a question to ask. Then, "What did Jesus say to the woman at the well in John, chapter four?"

Pages turn with a flurry. "I know! I know!" says one boy. Before the others find the passage, one reads aloud, "Jesus answered her, 'If you knew the gift of God and who it is that asks you for a drink, you would have asked him and he would have given you living water.' "

"Fantastic!" says Grandpa. "Good work!"

Good-natured "high fives" all around, and the boys get ready for the next one. Grandpa pretends he is trying to think of a tough one. He likes that part. He comes up with it and the race is on again. Grandpa's Bible Drill is fun after-dinner recreation and good training for these boys who love the Lord. There's always plenty of time to play in the California sunshine.

TEACHING ABOUT GOD'S UNIVERSE

Many who have graduated to grandparenting carry around thirty or forty years of experience in a career. Yours might be in forestry. His in aerospace. Hers in accounting. Mine in cooking. How about dredging up some of that knowledge, dusting it off, and sharing it with the grandkids?

Whenever ours spend an afternoon with Grandpa, they learn a little something, whether it is how to build a wooden toy or how his bulldozer runs or how God set the planets in order. My husband spent years as a newsman covering the early Mercury and Gemini launches into space from Cape Canaveral. Here is how Grandpa taught Jeremy at age eight on another day in his workshop:

"Many Very Energetic Men Just Sit Under Neath Pluto!" he said.

Jeremy's mouth fell open. "What did you say, Grandpa?"

"I just gave you the names of the planets in God's

universe, Jeremy, beginning with the one closest to the sun. And the easiest way I know to remember them. See here!"

Grandpa wrote on his chalkboard on the workshop wall:

Many	Very	Energetic	Men	Just	Sit	Under	Neath	Pluto
e	e	a		a	u	a	r	e	l
r	n	r		r	p	t	a	p	u
c	u	t		s	i	u	n	t	t
u	s	h			t	r	u	u	o
r					e	n	s	n	
y					r			e	

"The first one, Mercury, is closest to the sun. Pluto is the farthest from the sun."

Grandpa then erased the board and handed the chalk to Jeremy. "Now, you write it."

"Wow!" exclaimed Jeremy. With a little prompting from his grandpa, he repeated the acrostic and learned a lesson he has never forgotten.

Grandpa Endicott has also learned a lot about animals that inhabit the earth. One day he and Christopher visited the zoo.

At the lion's cage, the wide-eyed five-year-old watched as a zoo employee threw huge scraps of meat to the animals. Some of the males snarled at each other, trying to be first in line for dinner.

"See the carnivores!" said Grandpa.

"Huh? We're not at the carnival, Grandpa!"

"No, no. A carnivore eats meat," he explained carefully. "The lion is carnivorous. So is the dog, the wolf, the cat, the seal, and many others, including you and me. We're different from herbivores that eat only vegetation, like cows and horses. Let's sit over here for a while and talk about it."

Grandfather and grandson spent fifteen priceless min-utes on a park bench recalling the animals of the ark that went aboard two by two. Which ones were carnivorous and which ones were herbivorous?

These days, when Chris takes a break from his studies at college, he telephones his grandpa and challenges him to name more carnivorous and herbivorous animals than he can.

I hope you have experienced the exhilaration of times like these. The children never grow "too old" to learn from their grandpa. He never tires of trying to teach them something.

It's never too late to try.

SPECIAL OUTING

If Mountain Time with your grandchildren means taking them on a special outing, the following idea will help you combine learning with the fun of anticipation of the trip.

When each of my grandchildren reaches age three, it's time to "go tootin'" with Grandma. Then, once a year thereafter.

First, Grandma makes a date with the grandchild and gives advance notice to the parents. The child wears his or her Sunday best because "going tootin'" begins with lunch—not a fast lunch at McDonald's but at a favorite sit-down restaurant. At lunch, the child and Grandma look the menu over and the child orders from the waiter or waitress. Napkins are placed on laps. When lunch arrives, thank you's are said, and the child learns to eat with a fork and ask for salt or pepper, "please." After lunch, Grandma and child figure the tip, and Grandma gives the child money to pay the bill, after which thank you's are repeated.

Then, it's off to the mall for "two needs" and "one want."

The child's two needs are set ahead with the parents. They range from new jeans to a pair of tennis shoes to a Sunday white shirt and tie. The one "want" is the child's heart's desire, within reason; one thing he or she wants very much. It might be a bag of M and M's, a new pair of black party shoes, or the latest sports poster.

One time four-year-old Amy laid out ten things in the aisle of a busy toy store, then proceeded to eliminate them one by one to get down to the one she really wanted. Store clerks and customers walked around her for nearly a half hour.

If we have left a sibling at home, we always buy "some little thing" for them, something chosen by the child who is "tootin'." One time it took five-year-old Michelle twenty-five minutes to pick out "some little thing" for her baby brother, Stewart.

"Going tootin' " teaches manners that the child may or may not learn at home. It teaches the value of money; we discuss the cost of lunch as well as the price of the "two needs" and "one want." It teaches the difference between "wanting" and "needing," a valuable lesson for later years. The children love to "go tootin' " and I treasure each time, reliving the memory again and again.

So pack your patience and a word of advice: stick to the rules. Don't let your grandchild coerce you into more purchases or more expensive purchases. I set a limit of twenty dollars on the "two needs" and ten on the "one want." The "little something" for the sibling at home can cost as little as one dollar. It's just a token and that's important. Because the sibling will soon have his or her own turn.

Chris is now twenty. He recently asked when we're "going tootin'." My answer? "It's your turn to take me!"

THE PAST IS PAST

Just as we have much to teach our grandchildren, so we grandparents have much to learn.

Lee Loevinger, eighty-seven-year-old legal theorist and past supreme court justice of Minnesota, wrote in an essay on growing old, "There is a great difference, in my view, between those who are still growing and those who are old; the old are those who have stopped growing. You are old when you lose interest in learning."[2]

Learning to let go of the past is sometimes hard for a grandparent. Some of us carry guilt from our own parenting experiences that can seriously impact our Mountain Time. Do any of these sentiments ring true for you?

"If only I had been as good a father (or mother) as I am a grandparent."

"We never had enough money to give the children what they needed."

"I never had enough time because I had to work."

"If I hadn't demanded they go to church, maybe they would be going today."

"If I could turn back the clock, I would do things so differently."

Two realizations about my parenting years have blessed me greatly.

The first is that I did the best I could at the time. After my divorce, I carried a heavy burden of guilt. My four children and I had no financial support when we began our life as the "Fearsome Five." We had hope and love, love for each other and for the Lord.

What do my grown and successful children remember today?

• Not the shabby house in which we lived.
• Not the times we cooked hot dogs in the fireplace

60

because we couldn't pay the electric bill.

• Not the nights we huddled together in the cold.

No. They remember the good times.

• Racing their homemade cars down the steep driveway of our "shabby house."

• Whittling sticks for the hot dogs in the fireplace with their own knife.

• Snuggling together and tickling each other, giggling until they fell asleep in the cold.

The second realization hit me like a bolt of lightning as I listened to a radio program one day.

"God loves you just the way you are. But he loves you too much to leave you that way."

What a revelation! All of life is a growing and learning experience; even those stretching times we might like to forget or change are part of his perfect plan.

Leaving the past with the Lord makes me a better grandparent. I am free and I hope that you, too, will release the tarnished shackles of bad memories and unfulfilled expectations and lay them at the foot of the Cross where they belong. Then you, like the children, can keep on growing and learning.

He wants Mountain Time with you and he wants you to have it with your grandchildren.

Let God take you there. When you "look over" in the years to come, you will see the fruit in the vineyard and the view will astound you.

In divorce, we must remember that God is not absent, neither has he finished working in our children or our grandchildren. When divorce tears a family apart, we need help from God. He has a wondrous way of knowing how to love each one of us, from the smallest child to the senior Grandpa.

As we let him love us, we receive the grace to pass on to our grandchildren the exact things that will bring them through this experience stronger and more able to trust their heavenly Father.

Where there is chaos, he creates beauty. The ashes of our lives become the clay out of which he sculpts glory.

Barbara Cook

5
...

Grandparents of Divorce

As parents, our hopes and dreams were tied up in our children. We prayed they would grow up to be healthy, God-fearing, compassionate people who would marry healthy, God-fearing, compassionate people, have our grandchildren and live happily ever after. Not so for many of us in America today. The sad truth is that we have children raising children, parents aborting children, and parents stripping their children of a basic sense of security and safety.

Jesus said, "Only in his hometown and in his own house is a prophet without honor" (Matt. 13:57). We advise our children in hope of helping them avoid the mistakes we made. Sadly, that advice often falls on deaf ears. The consequences may affect the welfare, sometimes the very life, of a grandchild whose future hangs precariously and innocently in the balance.

Grandparenting Redefined

What can and should a grandparent do when the happy life of a precious little person who calls you Grandma or Grandpa is forever changed by divorce? What is our role when hopes and dreams come crashing down to the realities of incompatibility, dishonesty, and whatever else destroys what we thought was a happy marriage and the consequences fall on small shoulders? Like Sam's.

"FIXING IT"

Mike sat at one end of the child psychologist's desk. His wife, Melissa, sat as far as she could get at the other end. In between, sitting in his own "big-boy chair," was their four-year-old son, Sam. His little arms reached high to rest on the chair arms, and his fingers wiggled nervously as he stared at the doctor sitting behind the desk.

Mike shot a quick look at Melissa and adjusted his large frame in the chair. Melissa, sitting straight with one leg across the other, shot one of her own looks past Sam to his father. A look of anger and frustration. A look that screamed, "I don't love you anymore!"

Sam glanced from one parent to the other, hoping for some encouragement that whatever was happening would soon be over. He got none.

Mike broke the stiff silence. "Can we get on with this?"

"Well, Sam!" said the doctor. "How are you today?"

Sam, big and tall like his dad, and proud of his size, pulled his chest up and out and responded, "I'm tough!" His eyes sparkled and with a satisfied grin on his freckled face, he looked up at his dad, the former professional football player. He wanted approval from his father. And he got it. Their grins relaxed the tension in the room for just that moment and a soft, wistful smile crossed Melissa's face.

"Good, Sam!" The doctor settled back in his chair. "How do you feel now about your dad living in another place and you and your mom living in the house?"

"I don't like it! I want my daddy to come home!"

This time it was Melissa who shifted silently in her chair.

"Aren't you happy living with your mother?"

"Yes . . . but . . ."

"But what?"

"I want everything back together."

"You want everything back together? But you do understand that your mom and dad have decided they can't live together, don't you?"

"Yeah, but I'm gonna fix it so they can." Sam puffed two short, deep breaths in and out. "I'm gonna fix it!"

"Aha!" The doctor's voice lowered to a gentle, understanding tone, as if to try to help the little boy reconcile the fact of his parents' broken marriage.

"And how are you going to do that, Sam?"

Sam stopped puffing, looked first at his mother, a glow of new excitement and expectation illuminating his little face. Then at his dad, with a "Rocky II" confidence that he had the answer. He was going to win! But as he looked back at the psychologist who leaned forward waiting for an answer, Sam held his breath and, in an instant, the glow of childish pride and hope drained from his face. Then he abruptly jumped down from his chair, ran over to the doctor's couch, rolled up in the fetal position facing the wall and said softly, "I don't know."

Melissa is my daughter. Sam is my grandson. After Melissa's phone call describing this heartbreaking counseling session, the shortest sentence in the Bible held a powerful, new meaning for me.

"Jesus wept" (John 11:35).

I wept for days. For the fact that two terrific parents could not get along with each other. But mostly for Sam who would now live in a world divided, with Mom on one side and Dad on the other, himself in the middle, madly in love with both.

Knowing the trauma our grandchildren must endure at the time of divorce makes us cry out in pain as well. We want to "fix it." Whose fault is it? Who can we blame? Surely we can find a way to make the pain go away.

Amid the finality of divorce, grandparents, too, must deal with separation. One day we have a son-in-law, the next, we don't. One Christmas, we're celebrating together, the next, we're not. The new year's family calendar no longer reminds us of his birthday but when the day comes, we remember. Now the grandchildren come over only when our child has visitation rights. Nothing will ever be the same again. The longing to "fix it" doesn't go away.

Today, Sam is a well-adjusted seven-year-old, largely because of excellent cooperation and guidance from his mother and father. By providing consistent love and a Christian education, Mike and Melissa are proving that Sam's best interest is their goal. My job, as grandparent, is to pray without ceasing for Sam and his baby sister, Gabrielle, be here when they need me, and trust the rest to the Lord.

GOD IS SUFFICIENT

When I took my heartache over this divorce to God in prayer, he sent me to his Word and to some thoughtful and insightful books on getting through a child's divorce largely for the sake of the grandchildren. Loving, caring friends also comforted and advised me through the hardest times. What I learned may help you:

1. *Before, during, and after the divorce, let the parents focus on their troubles while you focus on the grandchild, who often feels he or she must face the future all alone.* Pray without ceasing for your grandchild.

2. *You may be the only Jesus your grandchild will ever see.* Offer to take the child to church, youth group meeting, or camp. Make opportunities to read the Bible together. Find passages that offer hope and encouragement the child can understand and relate to his or her life. These are Mountain Times of eternal value.

3. *Move and speak carefully around the parents, with sensitivity and tact.* Ask one or both of the parents how they have explained the divorce, and use that as your basis for any conversation.

4. *Listen.* In order to hear what a grandchild of divorce is saying, we must put our own prejudices, preconceived ideas, and agenda aside. Don't rush in to "fix it." Try to imagine what this little person is going through and put yourself in that place. Your grandchild's perception of things will differ from yours.

5. *Affirm your grandchild's value often.* Build self-esteem at every opportunity.

6. *Never speak against either parent; blaming confuses and further alienates the child.* The child loves both parents and needs a safe place to express that love. Your blame may squelch the child's honest feelings so that expression of those feelings is not possible, making the needed feedback and acceptance impossible, as well. He or she may think, "If I say anything good about my daddy, Grandma will be mad at me, so I won't say anything." The child fears losing your love; it's one of the only constants left.

7. *Recognize and understand mood changes.* Joy at seeing you can turn in a flash to deep and pervasive sorrow which in fifteen minutes can change to anger and frustration. The world has cracked at the foundation and everything is unstable. You can be a haven where your grandchild feels accepted, free to talk and be open, unafraid to express honest feelings. Warning: keeping your grandchild's

confidence is critical to an ongoing environment of trust and sharing.

8. *Play with your grandchild.* Have fun together.

9. *Keep your normal routine at home when the child visits.* Your home may be the only one that hasn't changed. Visiting with you is a return to normalcy. You represent stability and family in an upside-down world.

10. *Make yourself available to baby-sit, especially if the child is latchkey.* Mountain Time with your grandchild includes contributing to safety.

11. *Offer assurance that the divorce was not your grandchild's fault, that conflict exists in all relationships.* Say very little, only when asked. Avoid analysis. Be honest but brief.

12. *Assure your grandchild of your love often.* This reinforces the ongoing stability of your relationship.

13. *Join a support group for grandparents of divorce where you can talk with others going through similar circumstances.* If you don't know of a support group for grandparents, start one. You won't have to look far to find a partner.

14. *Take care of your health in order to better serve your grandchildren.* Body defenses break down without proper nutrition, rest, exercise, and relaxation.

15. *When couples divide, let your love multiply.* "Hatred stirs up dissension, but love covers over all wrongs" (Prov. 10:12).

BE READY

From a study of 131 children of divorced families by Judith S. Wallerstein and Jean Berlin Kelly, here are some questions commonly asked by grandchildren of divorce, followed by my own comments:

1. *Who will take care of me?* Children of divorce can

70

have a profound sense of abandonment, loss, and rejection. Their trust in adults may be shattered. They worry that they may be abandoned by everyone, even their grandparents.

2. *Is there anything in the world that is reliable and predictable?* "And they lived happily ever after" is the ending of some stories read to children. They know the phrase well. Divorce can change that forever.

3. *Are my parents crazy?* When a marriage is falling apart, children see and hear things they shouldn't. They see their parents who individually express love to them, expressing hate and anger to each other.

4. *Where is my father/mother now living?* The absent parent was always there before. Where is he or she now?

5. *Will my father/mother (missing parent) get sick, hit by a car or worse?* Fear for the safety of the missing parent is common, especially if the child does not see him or her for long periods of time. Absence breeds worry.

6. *Will we have enough money now?* Even very little ones can exhibit concern about money. Some have heard too many arguments on the subject. Others have been denied their needs and wants.

7. *Will I have to change schools?* Disruption of the home signals fears of disruption at school.

8. *Will I have to move to a new neighborhood?* Everything is different now. Will I live in a different place, too, away from my friends?

9. *Is Mom going to marry somebody else?* Will they keep me? Will somebody take my daddy's place? Will he like me?[1]

Grandchildren may or may not verbalize such fears, but they are there, sometimes deep inside, screaming to get out and sometimes just under the surface, exploding without warning. Grandparents who listen without preaching, who reassure their grandchild in all circumstances, who

71

build rather than tear down, can bring order to the chaos a
loved one is living through.

BINDING THE TIE

Today we realize that members of the extended family
suffer the trauma of a divorce just as much as the spouse
and children involved. As the grandparents, our lives have
received a jolt and we undergo a terrible strain. Perhaps
worst of all, we have absolutely no control over the situation or the end results of other's choices.

We can, however, control our reactions to the situation
and the choices of others. We can choose to lay the emotional baggage at the foot of the Cross where it belongs
and leave it there. We can yell and scream our feelings out
to God.

Once we are empty and have given it *all* over to our
faithful Father, he will show the way to choices we can
live with.

Laurene Johnson and Georglyn Rosenfeld, in *Divorced
Kids*, say:

> Grandparents frequently suffer as much as the non-
> custodial parents because they have little or no con-
> tact with their grandchildren— particularly if they do
> not live in the same area. When the family unit was
> intact, the children may have spent vacations with
> them, but after the divorce, visitation requirements
> place the priority on the non-custodial parent.
>
> For years, much emotional carnage was left in the
> wake of a system that was accustomed to promoting
> only the interests of the feuding parents. Now, how-
> ever, nearly every state has laws guaranteeing the
> visitation rights of grandparents. And pending legis-
> lation may serve to promote those rights even further.

Clearly, it is in the best interests of all parties to allow continuing contact between grandparents and grandchildren, keeping the fabric of the family as intact as possible.[2]

"Be strong and courageous. . . . Do not be afraid or discouraged, for the Lord God, my God, is with you" (1 Chron. 28:20). David's words to Solomon as he built the temple are cornerstones of behavior for release from grandparenting grief because of your child's divorce. Can you imagine any cracks in Solomon's temple?

Be strong and courageous—and patient as you build a bridge to your grandchild. "He will not fail you or forsake you" (1 Chron. 28:20).

SAYING GOODBYE

I remember one unforgettable, but forgivable night, the last time I would see two of my beloved grandchildren for a long, long time. Divorce was ripping them away from us. The mother was taking her children across the country early the next morning. I remember holding my granddaughter in my arms on that awful night. She cried so hard. So did I. Neither of us knew what to say. All we could force out was "Write to me. I love you." The pain of their leaving lived in the nooks and crannies of my heart until I decided to allow the Holy Spirit to take it away and replace it with hope.

In the following weeks, God in his mercy showed me, day by day, that he was in control of the circumstances and that he would take care of me and those I love so dearly. "Cast all your anxiety upon him because he cares for you" (1 Pet. 5:7).

I began to heal and learn that goodbye doesn't necessarily mean forever.

God loves you. He loves your family. Every piece of your family's puzzle is important to him. But if the pieces of your family are lost or bent, surrender your puzzle to him.

Since Adam, God has worked in spite of man's independent personality. Put God in charge and he'll make a new picture. His picture.[1]

Michelle Cresse

6
...
Grandparents of Remarriage

Once the divorce involving a grandchild is final, time goes by and something called a "normal routine" is re-established. But then an announcement of remarriage brings us grandparents a whole new set of prayer concerns.

First of all, the news is usually a shock, happy or sad. Siblings and friends will hear about it before we do. Certainly, in this day and age, we're rarely consulted. Our parenting season is basically over when the child marries. We are often on the fringe of our divorced child's life, clutching the moniker "extended family member" as our only claim to credibility. Even if we are asked for advice before the marriage, that advice will probably fall on ears that only hear what they want to hear and a heart that's in love. As my Norwegian uncle used to say, "Ven luf comes in da door, da brains go out da vindow!"

OUR NEED TO KNOW

We know that the great majority of those who divorce, remarry at least once. Grandparents ask a number of questions before the new marriage:

1. *What kind of stepparent will this new daughter- or son-in-law be?* When a divorced child has dated the intended for a while, grandparents may have an opportunity to get to know the person and form some opinions about sincerity, honesty, and parenting potential. If danger signals appear, especially if they reveal a threat to the welfare of the grandchild, the grandparent has a responsibility to speak up, asked or not. An early warning could avert a tragedy. Be brave. You have a right to ask questions of those entrusted with the future of your grandchild.

2. *Will my grandchildren like the new stepmom or stepdad?* Psychologists tell us that kids of divorce are hungry for the absent parent's love and attention. They are innocently attracted to a show of affection by the prospective stepparent. Such a child is vulnerable to a false sense of security and can expect far more from the new parent than is reasonable, leading sometimes to deep disappointment and emotional trauma to all parties. Grandparents can stabilize this situation by encouraging the child to be patient and understanding. We also make excellent listening ports in a storm.

3. *Will the new couple have enough money to adequately care for the child(ren)?* "Enough money" is a misnomer. Some second marriages need little money if deeper needs are met: love, sharing, working together as a family toward goals. And if they are short of money, it's their problem, not yours. They'll work it out without your help, and you'll be the first to know if they need it. (See chapter 12.)

4. *Does the newcomer care about my grandchildren?*
Will my grandchildren be neglected when new ones are
born to this couple? In light of the horrifying statistics on
child abuse, this is a logical question. How can we tell?
The truth is, we can't. But we can be alert, watch, and
listen. And we can get involved in our grandchild's life.
Eighty percent of divorced women in America remarry
one or more times, leaving a lot of children who were sure
that the first one was the right one, wondering, as they
grow up, who they can trust. Let your grandchild see you
as an example of consistency, someone to talk to if things
go sour.

5. *Will I like the children being brought into this new
marriage? Will they call me Grandma?* Every child is
unique before God. I've always thought, when referring to
a remarriage, that words like "blended" and "reconsti-
tuted" sound more like orange juice than human beings.
Every new family will be different. The children brought
into the new family are a challenge for every member of
the existing family—on both sides. Just remember that
nowhere is it written that you have to like them! You
probably will! Maybe you won't.

My friend, author/counselor Jean Lush, advises that
you'll save yourself a lot of grief if you don't try to
pretend that you like or love the new kids. Give it time. Be
honest about your feelings and let God work on the relationship. He's known for his miracles.

6. *Will the newcomer nurture my grandchild's spiritual
faith?* Sometimes going to church, family devotions, and
praying drop to the bottom of the "to do" list when a
young couple is busy building a "new life together" with
ready-made children. Just as you did during and after the
divorce, offer to take the child to church, a youth group
meeting, or camp. You can stand in the gap for your

grandchild as a Christ-like example and keep the child's faith strong and growing.

7. *Will they move away?* If the newcomer is from out of state, this concern moves up to Number One. Keep in mind that you have no control over that decision; you can only control your response if it happens. Chapter 11 offers some creative ideas on how to strengthen the bond with your grandchildren when they live far away. (I haven't come up with a way to fix the ache in our hearts from missing them, though.)

8. *How will my relationship with my grandchild change?* When a divorced child takes a new partner, that change may affect when and where you see your grandchild(ren), when and if you share meals with them, and some of the plans you may have established for them before the new marriage. This is especially true if your child has been a single parent for a matter of years; you have a set pattern in your relationship with your grandchildren.

Sometimes grandparents are drawn closer into the family after their son's or daughter's remarriage. Sometimes we find ourselves feeling outside the circle, a little less a part of the new family than of the old. Be patient. Their agenda is full, particularly in the beginning. This is one of those times for which God allowed us to grow older. We are supposed to be wise and understanding by now, by his grace.

If indeed remarriage means the family moves away, look for a huge change in your relationship with the grand-child. In a new area, the child will have new friends, a new school. You are a part of that new environment from afar as well as an important family link to the past. The child needs that to maintain a sense of family in a new and different place.

Your relationship with your grandchildren may hinge on your acceptance of these changes. Properly handled, change can draw you and your grandchildren even closer through creative expressions of long distance love. (See chapter 11.)

ACCEPTING THE NEW

Remarriage of our grandkids' mom or dad brings another unique dilemma of acceptance: How can we accept this new person when we still love (and miss) the old one? This is a difficult assignment for some and causes a roller coaster of emotions. The guilt! In my own case, how can I accept our new daughter-in-law without feeling disloyal to the first one, who was an integral part of our lives for twelve years? I'm angry that we are even faced with such a choice and still a little bitter and resentful that the divorce happened in the first place.

Who is this new person? How could I possibly care about her when I love my ex-daughter-in-law so much?

Well, guess what? I do! You can't *not* love Valerie, who is the kindest, most thoughtful, lovely woman you'd ever want as your daughter-in-law. She loves my stepson, our two grandchildren, and she's given us grandchild number eleven—Olivia!

But what about my relationship with the "ex"? Sure, it hurt the first time she called me Irene instead of "Mom." And at Christmas, Easter, and her birthday, my cards aren't to "a dear daughter-in-law" anymore but to "a special friend." I have learned, though, that I can nurture the old relationship just as I nurture the new. I don't have to lose this loved one. It's a win/win situation if I handle it properly and prayerfully with understanding and patience.

Most importantly, it's okay to feel the honest emotions of anger, profound sadness, and loss. It's healthy to acknowledge, express, and then pray about them.

A CHILD'S VIEW

My friend Mary's daughter and son-in-law got one of those so-called "amicable" divorces resulting in joint custody. The ex-son-in-law remarried and all parties attended the grandmother's church. One Sunday, Mary's daughter brought the little girl to church; the next Sunday the ex-son-in-law and his new wife brought her. Upon seeing her grandmother, the child's face reflected her confusion.

"Is it okay to say hello to my grandma? I'm with my daddy today."

Or, on Sundays with her mother: "There's my daddy over there on that side and there's my grandma on the other. Should I talk to them? Should I even smile at them?"

Mary dealt with this unusual situation by asking both parents to explain to the child in clear terms what was expected of her when she encountered her mother, father, and/or grandmother in church. She has since noticed her granddaughter is much more relaxed. Communication and cooperation are the keys.

GIVE IT AWAY

An adult child's remarriage can bring a blessed stability to that child's life, sometimes after a long, singular struggle for emotional and financial good health. A strong and healthy second marriage can also signal a new beginning for a grandchild who now has a renewed sense of security and belonging. Loving grandparents play an important role in this process. The grandparent is the root or the core of the family. We are not "divorced" from the child nor are we a part of the "remarriage." We can try to be there, nurturing, understanding, and ready to listen, no matter what happens in the child's life. What a privilege! What a responsibility!

Grandparents of Remarriage

Some remarriages bring heartaches. We may not like the new person or the new person doesn't care for us. The grandchild may have to move away. Whatever happens, as much as we would like to, we can't change the circumstances nor should we judge others in the family. Give it away.

Dear God,
Bless this union. Help me to be the grandparent you want me to be. Thank you for everything you are going to do for this family. May my grandchild see you through me.
Amen

When you've forgiven "seventy times seven" in only one week, and when you've come to the end of your rope and tied a knot so many times that your rope looks like a string of rugged pearls, you come to know the amazing reality of God's promises: "My strength is sufficient" and "My power shows up best in weak people."

Gloria Gaither

7
...

Parenting
All Over Again

In no other way is the change in grandparenting so graphically and tragically lived out than in the lives of grandparents raising grandchildren. Exhibiting the kind of courage only God can give, grandparents today are taking legal custody of their grandchildren and becoming parents all over again.

The lights were on, but the room was dark on a dreary winter day in Seattle. Silent shadows danced on the walls as Grandma and Grandpa arrived with the attorneys. Grandpa held three-year-old Nicholas in his arms.

As they found a place to sit and put the papers down, Nicholas' daddy walked into the room. He looked thin, his mother thought, but then Kevin had looked that way for a long, long time. How she ached to have the real Kevin back, the one the family used to know, before the cocaine, the failed rehabilitations, the abuse, and the jail sentences.

Grandparenting Redefined

As much as she hated what had happened, she knew her mother's heart showed in her eyes as they met Kevin's. A mother's love for her son reached across the small room, and she wished things were different.

But she could shed no more tears. She had cried rivers over the months of torment, the sleepless nights worrying about Kevin behind the wheel of a car, wondering whether he would be fired from his job, wondering if Nadine would come home from another three-day binge, wondering if Nicholas were safe. She knew what she was doing was right. This mother had run out of excuses for her son's and daughter-in-law's behavior. For two years she had tried to help them kick the substance abuse habits that had brought them to this day and this place.

Head bowed, Daddy Kevin sat down at the other end of the long table, casting a weak wave to his little son. Nicholas' big brown eyes were fixed on his father, expressionless. He made no move toward him as he twisted his grandpa's tie around his hand.

Grandpa stared vacantly at one worn spot on the table.

This was it, the day fifty-two-year-old Grandma and Grandpa Kiley would take legal custody of Nicholas. All that remained was the arrival of Nicholas' mother, Nadine, and everybody's signatures on the dotted line.

Nadine burst through the door, with an unlit cigarette in one hand and car keys in the other. She looked straight ahead, ignoring the presence of anyone else in the room. *Probably coming down from another high*, thought her mother-in-law. Nadine's hands shook as she pulled out a chair and slumped down, sprawling her legs as if she couldn't care less about these proceedings.

She didn't even look at Nicholas.

Grandpa turned to her as though he wanted to ask a question. Perhaps, "How could you let it come to this?"

Or, "How could you leave Nicholas alone for three days?" Or, "Do you understand, we *have* to do this?" His wife's hand on his caused him to lean back. The time for questions and answers had passed.

The lawyer cleared his throat, breaking the awkward silence, and in monotone, began to explain the proceedings:

"This is a legal proceeding in the state of Washington, King County, for the purpose of transferring custody of Nicholas Adam Kiley to his grandparents, Dorothy Ellen Kiley and James Richard Kiley with the signed consent of the child's parents, Nadine Marie and Kevin James Kiley. . . ."

One by one, pen and papers were passed around the table.

Kevin picked up the pen and affixed a sloppy signature to each page. He stood up without a word, softly touched his mother's shoulder as he tousled Nicholas' curly hair, and walked quickly out of the room.

Nadine, who had barely made it through the attorney's explanation, grabbed the pen. She signed the papers, stood up, and after one burning glance at Grandma Kiley, stomped out of the room.

Dotty and Jim were now the legal parents of their three-year-old grandson.

Little Nicholas looked up at his grandmother and asked, "Are you my mommy now?"

As they left the room, Dotty said to the attorney, "Pray with me that someday we will have to give him back."

This tragic scene, in many different settings, is repeated daily in hundreds of American cities. "Good Christian kids," who, like Kevin, grew up with advantages, strong support, and opportunities to succeed, have become dysfunctional parents. And grandparents who have raised their own children, and earned the time and money for themselves and their dreams, are potty training and seeing to their grandchildren's financial, emotional, spiritual, and physical needs—parenting all over again.

Why is this happening?

Substance abuse is by far the number one cause of grandparents' legal custody of their grandchildren. Others are:

- death by illness, accident, or suicide
- neglect
- abandonment
- incarceration
- physical, emotional, and/or sexual abuse
- mental illness [1]

FACING THE ISSUES

Sylvie deToledo is a licensed clinical social worker at the Psychiatric Clinic for Youth in Long Beach, California. In 1987, an informal survey at the clinic revealed that approximately ten percent of the clients were living in homes where grandparents were the parents. She announced a new support group for these grandparents and, to her shock, seventy-five people showed up at the first meeting. She leads four such groups today. DeToledo says grandparents as parents deal with numerous issues.

The ages of the grandparents in our groups range from early 40's to late 70's. They are raising children from infants to adolescents, from all socio-economic levels and ethnic groups. Some feel alone and isolated, knowing no one in the same situation. Several lack the support of a helpful family or may have few, if any, friends who understand their new situation. Some have to stop working to raise their grandchildren. All are dealing with heavy emotional, relational issues, while finding it difficult, at best, to have their own needs met or continue the activities they once participated in and enjoyed.[2]

THE "GRAND" IS GONE

Most grandparents interviewed admit to kaleidoscopic feelings of anger, grief, and self-pity. However, the overriding emotion is love. Grandparents want to see their grandchildren kept together, not separated and placed into foster homes. They want the best for their grandchildren. Counselor deToledo hears it daily:

These grandparents see that they cannot make up for what the children have not had in the past but can work on the here and now of building a foundation of trust, love and security. Some are targets of the grandchildren's anger and, at times, rage they feel toward their own parents. Some are in a constant struggle to maintain a life of their own while raising grandchildren who have a deep sense of insecurity and demand attention. It has been my experience that, where there is a grandfather in the home, he tends to be viewed by the children as the more authoritarian figure, whereas the grandmother is more easily manipulated. Frequently, the grandparents have conflicting ideas about the way the children should be dealt with, creating a divisive attitude toward the situation. This may result in Grandmother overcompensating for the stern attitude of the husband. Grandfathers may feel deprived or neglected by their wives and retreat to their own activities, distancing themselves from the family situation. This brings resentment from Grandmother who experiences the burden of raising the children almost single-handedly. Some long-standing marriages end in divorce.

We stress sharing the responsibilities. It is also imperative that grandparents be encouraged to set time aside for themselves away from the grandchildren, a time when they can give to each other, to emotionally refill themselves and their relationship.[3]

Grandparents often complain, deToledo says, of being "robbed" of the traditional role of "doting" grandparents. Conversely, children are often deprived of the type of affection usually lavished by their grandparents. These grandparents are now "parents" and these grandchildren are "children." The "grand" is taken out of these roles by virtue of the circumstances.

Grandparents with health problems, such as poor vision and arthritis, find their own care taking a backseat to the needs of the grandchildren. Counselors say poverty fuels the fire as some grandmothers will pay forty to fifty dollars for shoes for the grandchild and they will wear three-dollar shoes themselves.

A GROWING DILEMMA

The 1990 Census reports that 3,155,000 of America's children live in a home maintained by their grandparent(s), an increase from the 2,306,000 reported in 1980. That's five percent of all children under eighteen years of age. Today, fifteen percent of children living with grandparents also have both parents living with them; fifty percent have only their mother present; and thirty percent are cared for by only the grandparents. Between 1980 and 1990, the proportion of these children living with only their mother increased. Black children are more likely to live in their grandparents' home (twelve percent of all Black children under eighteen) than are White children (four percent). Black children living in their grandparents' home also are more likely to be living with only the grandparents (thirty-eight percent compared with twenty-five percent of White grandchildren). Among children of Hispanic origin, six percent live in the home of their grandparents and twenty-one percent of these grandchildren live with only their grandparents.[4]

David Liederman, executive director of the Child Welfare League of America, says that it's not new that grandparents have stepped in to take care of grandchildren, but that it has increased at a more than normal rate because of the tremendous increase in drug-related problems.

How are these grandparents coping with unplanned parenthood?

As the number of grandparents raising their grandchildren increases, so does the number of support groups in America. Sylvie deToledo's organization in Long Beach, California is named Grandparents As Parents (GAP). The goals of GAP are:

• to reduce stress felt by grandparents raising grandchildren.

• to develop a support network between these grandparents.

• to provide the opportunity to verbalize and share feelings and unique issues grandparents as parents face, in a warm, supportive environment. Topics include anger toward their children for shirking parental responsibility; resentment toward grandchildren; feelings of missing out on being *grandparents*; and positive feelings and experiences of grandparenting.[5]

YOU CAN HELP

Another leading support/advocacy group is Second Time Around Parents in Media, Pennsylvania. Licensed social worker Michele Daly leads this group whose objectives are:

• To help grandparents obtain foster parent funds without gaining custody of the grandchildren.

• To provide funding for educational and therapeutic programs for the grandchildren.

• To offer financial and emotional support services to grandparents, as well as assistance with legal rights and custody issues.

• To seek funding for a national grandparent support network and to assist with the initiation of new groups.

Sharing and discussion forums are held on such topics as custody, financial support, parent visits, community resources and grandparent issues.[6]

Counselors say the church is lagging way behind in providing a nurturing environment for grandparents with custody of their grandchildren. Perhaps the problem is relatively new and the magnitude of the numbers are just now surfacing as fact.

I have provided a list of support groups nationwide and other grandparenting resources in the back of this book. If you know of a need in your church, why not be the one to start a group? So often we think of the "church" as "they." "Why don't 'they' do something?" In this case, as in so many others, "they" is "us." If you decide to begin a grandparenting support group in your church, grandmas and grandpas all around you will come forward to join.

Counselor deToledo says the characteristics exhibited by children who have been molested can vary from mild to heartbreaking. She tells me these little ones who have been physically or sexually assaulted can react by sexually acting out, regressing to earlier stages of development, withdrawing or rebelling, and running away. Other symptoms of abuse include depression, fear of the dark, nightmares, difficulty falling asleep, changes in eating patterns, anxiety, overly sophisticated sexual knowledge, poor peer relationships, and enuresis (bed-wetting). These symptoms are a child's way of expressing what they cannot verbalize.[7]

A number of these grandchildren are hyperactive and under medication to control this condition. Such children tend to manifest their symptoms behaviorally, both at home and at school. They have trouble concentrating, difficulty following directions, are impulsive and easily distracted. They can hardly sit still and are frequently disruptive. They often have trouble focusing on and completing their work in school. As a result, they feel like "bad children" and have low self-esteem. They require constant supervision, an exhaustive task for grandparents who have neither the energy nor the patience they once had.

Although these children are quite attached to their grandparents, for some it has not been an easy adjustment. They have a profound sense of abandonment, loss, and rejection by their parents. Because their sense of trust in adults who should have been trustworthy has been shattered, they worry, consciously or unconsciously, that they may be abandoned once again, this time by their grandparents.

Some grandparents assume that distancing the grandchild from the people and places that are a reminder of past anguish is best. However, counselors warn grandparents that *total* separation from the parent(s) is traumatic for the child. Revisiting the parents and neighborhood at least provides a link to reality. Never again seeing those people and places adds to stress.

Kids whose parents have torn them out of their environment feel it is their fault. In counseling, they come up with all kinds of reasons . . . "If I were a better kid, this wouldn't have happened."

95

As previously discussed, these children resist talking about their real feelings for fear their grandparents might be mad at them.

GRANDPARENTS COPING

The range of emotional involvement is staggering to grandparents raising grandchildren. Those who have placed their trust in God have a measure of peace as they fight the battles. Following are some heartrending stories of Christian grandparents coping with their new assignments.

Diane Werner is a grandparent and one of the founders of the Second Time Around Parents group in Pennsylvania. Diane was fired from her forty-two thousand dollar-a-year job after missing too much work because of the constant crises with her crack-addicted daughter. Diane is raising her six-year-old grandson and signs over her welfare checks so her grandson can attend a nonprofit, private school that Diane describes as "what Montessori was supposed to be in the beginning."

An outspoken advocate on behalf of grandparents who face a lack of financial and social support in their new parenting role, Diane was the 1990 recipient of the J.C. Penney "Spirit of the American Woman" award.

When we spoke together, Diane's twenty-four-year-old daughter, unmarried, was "supposedly off drugs and pregnant again in Florida."

"I miss her something awful," Diane admitted, "but it's hard to hold out a lot of hope for her future. She keeps falling back into the old patterns. My prayer is simply that she might have a peaceful life and can someday enjoy being a mother as I did. Her son doesn't want to see her or talk to her. I teach him that there are all kinds of people in the world and that we don't have to like everyone—that's God's job."

She goes on to say, "I've never been happier in my life than now with legal custody of my grandson. You see, I know he's all right. I have peace of mind about that, and the times I have with him are treasures. Plus, I get to help so many other grandparents in the same boat."[8]

Albert and Mary Etta Johnson are raising grandchildren aged nine and eight while their daughter battles addiction to alcohol, cocaine, and heroin. Despite the burdens, Mr. Johnson, who has suffered two heart attacks and twice undergone open heart surgery, says they have no choice but to give their grandchildren a good home until their daughter can care for them. The Johnsons admit they don't have the energy, patience, or stamina they used to have, but they love their grandchildren.

Mary Etta said, "I couldn't have lived with myself if I hadn't taken them! There was no one else. We paid a lot of money even before our daughter's divorce. They'd ask and we'd give it to them, not knowing it was going for drugs. They learned to lie, cheat, and steal to get drugs. We spent a great deal of money to get the guardianship so they can't take these kids and put them through any more.

"I am so angry that drugs have robbed these little kids of their parents and us of the role of grandparents as God intended. Social service systems, police departments, and the courts are in critical need of education on this issue of grandparents raising their grandkids. We are given the cold shoulder when we need help.

"I'm from a family of twelve and our dear mother taught us that God does not give us more than we can handle. I truly believe that. When I think I have problems, I just look at what another grandparent is going through, and I think 'I don't have it so bad.' Each day brings a new set of problems or a new set of joys. We cried with our daughter at the celebration of her first year of sobriety.

Now, she's been sober fourteen months. We have hope."[9]

Candy Johnson cares for her eighty-two-year-old invalid mother and three grandsons, twins, eight, and an eleven-year-old. Candy had five miscarriages during her parenting years. She has one child, a daughter who has never married and is the mother of the three grandchildren. When Candy's daughter was first pregnant with the twins, she planned to have an abortion. Candy pleaded with her, saying abortion is against the will of God and aided her daughter through the pregnancy. After much hardship, when the twins were eighteen-months-old, social workers told Candy that if she couldn't take them, they would be sent to a children's home. Lying in bed that night, struggling with her decision, Candy listened to the radio.

"A report came on that the very children's home my twin grandchildren were to be placed in was under investigation for child abuse. That was like a sign from the Lord that I was to take them. I've had the older boy since he was four and the twins more than six years now, and I really feel like the Lord returned three of the ones I lost so many years ago."

Candy quit her job to care for the children. She moved from an apartment to a big house. Aid for Dependent Children funds are inadequate to meet her ever-rising expenses, and the demands of her mother and the grandchildren are exhausting. But she says, "I can take it. I go to my grandparent support group meetings and that helps a lot. At least I know my grandchildren are safe. I know in my heart that this is the right thing to do."[10]

Melody Hudgins is raising her own two children, ages eight and seventeen, plus her six-year-old grandson. Melody's sister keeps her five-year-old granddaughter and another two-year-old granddaughter lives in a foster home. Melody's daughter, the children's mother, is in and out of jail for drug-related charges, plus running away from a prison work furlough program.

"I pray a lot," Melody says, "to control my anger. I pray for strength and patience, and I pray for my grandchildren. I can only take care of one, and when I got him four years ago, he was a wild child who had seen too much. I go to a grandparent support group and get my anger out. Friends at my church pray with me and for me and my grandson.

"My grandson is settled and doing fine, but when my daughter visits, he reverts to his old ways of bed-wetting, tantrums, and disobedience. But my God told me he will never leave me or forsake me. We've come a long way. We take it one day at a time together. A lot of grandparents out there are in worse shape than I because they don't know the Lord." [11]

Pat Smith's only daughter, Karyn, gave her six grandchildren without benefit of marriage. One father was white, the other was black. Karyn was unable to pay the rent and began to abuse alcohol. Pat brought three of the children into her home for several years. Then Karyn remarried and took all six children to live in another state to make a new start.

"It was hard for Karyn," Pat says. "The kids were called 'Oreos' and 'Zebras.'"

Karyn and the six children returned home to live with Grandma. "It was that or foster homes for the kids, and I couldn't stand the thought. Karyn started drinking heavily, probably due to depression. She got no help from the fathers of the children and little from the state."

Pat raised the six children for eight years while her daughter tried to get her life straightened out. In 1986, Karyn married a man who took all six kids (none his own) and is raising them with love and compassion. All of the children adore him and call him Papa.

"It hurt to let them go back, but I was tired. I'm disabled, diabetic, and have fallen and broken my legs. So I felt sorry for myself sometimes, sure. But, my prayer was always for my daughter, that she would straighten out her life and be able to take care of her children. God has answered my prayer. I have peace."

Remember Nicholas at the beginning of this chapter? After the legal custody signing, three-year-old Nicholas looked at his grandmother and asked, "Are you my mommy now?"

"No, Nicholas," Dotty answered. "I am your grandma and your mother is your mommy. You are coming to live with your grandma and your grandpa and we love you very much."

Dotty has never regretted those words. Her son, Kevin, has been drug-free for two years and is about to marry a woman Dotty and Jim like very much. The grandparents have relinquished legal custody of Nicholas, now five, to his father. They have real hope that the new family will succeed.

Dotty had asked her attorney and others to pray with her that someday they would *have* to give Nicholas up. "We prepared ourselves at the outset that this could be a long-term or a short-term relationship," Dotty says. "Our interest has always been what's best for Nicholas. His grandpa and I used to tuck him into bed at night. We'd get on our knees and praise God before saying our prayers. Nicholas would pray for the whole clan and, if Grandpa was traveling, for his protection. Then, we'd sing a lullaby together:

Lullaby and good night.

Go to bed now and sleep tight.

Close your eyes and start to yawn.

Pleasant dreams until the dawn.

"Dawn has come for Nicholas and his daddy."

"I taught Nicholas the song, 'I Am A Promise' and he loves to sing it:

I am a promise
I am a possibility
I am a promise with a capital "P"
I am a great big bundle of potentiality!
I am learning to hear God's voice
I am trying to make the right choice.
I am a promise to be
Anything God wants me to be.[12]

"Nicholas will be all right now. We just praise the Lord for his great goodness and mercy."

Researching this chapter has touched my soul. I thank the Lord for the strength, courage, and love that he alone provides grandparents who find themselves parenting all over again. The true stories told here can be multiplied by hundreds. Somehow, even though I myself am not in this mixed-blessing situation with any of my twelve grandchildren, I relate with deep compassion to each story.

Will you join with me in praise and adoration of our sovereign God whose plan it is that we are living? And will you add your own prayer for all those grandparents in trouble who are not yet leaning on the Lord?

To the grandparent who *can* relate to the case histories shared:

• Please seek help *now*. The laws are changing, thanks to activist groups. There is support for you. You do have the right of petition when your grandchild's well-being is at stake.

• Speak up. For the child's sake and your own.

• Keep a diary of your circumstances. Many grandparents told me that a daily diary helped keep dates and facts straight prior to and during court action.

• Ask questions. Find out the differences between

transitional custody (guardianship), permanent custody, and adoption. Protect yourself.

• If friends tell you they know of something destructive going on in your adult child's life that affects your grandchild, have them sign a written declaration. They can even use a pseudonym if they are wary of signing their own name. It may hold as much weight in a court of law.

• Call the published 800-number in your state for a list of your legislator's committee assignments. Write your concerns to those lawmakers serving on child and family committees. Some of those concerns might be your perceived need for assistance to or revision of Child Protective Services in your area; or perhaps new legislation for financial aid to grandparents raising grandchildren.

• Check with your local NARCANON or ALANON organizations to see if they sponsor a grandparenting support group.

• Ask yourself whether or not, by helping your grandchildren's parents when they ask for it, you are *enabling* them. If you are an innocent "enabler," you can stop contributing to the problem by seeking professional assistance.

• Remember that grandparents parenting again is not a family secret any more. Get help!

"See, I am doing a new thing! Now it springs up; do you not perceive it? I am making a way in the desert and streams in the wasteland" (Isa. 43:19).

God the Father is our final Court of Appeals and he has the power to reverse decisions. "The king's heart is in the hand of the Lord; he directs it like a watercourse wherever he pleases" (Prov. 21:1).

Our loving Father may or may not choose to change our circumstances, but he can always change *us* through our circumstances. Either way, by faith we win.

Helene Ashker

8

...

Grandparents' Rights

Tina Scher is a Seattle-area grandparent who leads a grandparent support group as one who has "been there." Interviewed nationally, Tina and her husband, George, tell a wrenching story of their daughter's abandonment of her son. The Schers gained legal custody, and their daughter continues years of therapy for her self-destructive pattern of drug addiction.

Tina and George, however, feel blessed by what has happened. Their refreshing attitude is apparent as they take the hits of disappointment, time after time.

"Scripture tells us 'a little child shall lead them.' Well, our grandson is leading us. Because of him, we have a whole new way of thinking about ourselves and our lives. Our daughter allowed this to happen, but we're grateful that we can pick up the pieces. After all this time, our daughter is still not self-reliant. If that never changes, we have our grandson until he is nineteen. He has added so much to our lives. I just want to reach out with hope and resources to all those grandparents who don't feel this joy." [1]

Tina needed support herself, but she also wanted to reach out to grandparents in similar circumstances. She called Sharron Kick, community education director for Stevens Hospital in Edmonds, Washington, who responded enthusiastically to Tina's request for space to hold a meeting. A call to *The Seattle Times* and *The Everett Herald* resulted in front-page newspaper stories. The word spread and 110 grandparents showed up at the first meeting.

I was invited to attend a meeting; one I will never forget.

The attendees spent the first hour voicing individual concerns. Some couples looked too young to be grandparents, and some looked too old to take on the responsibility. Some had obvious medical problems. Married and single grandparents told heartbreaking tales of overwork, emotional stress, and financial hardship. Most expressed anger toward their adult child or an unresponsive system. Some spoke of feeling all alone in their situation. All exhibited profound sadness about their circumstances and a mixture of fear and anxiety about the future. For that hour, they knew, perhaps for the first time, that others could relate to their experience. Love from Tina's caring heart and other grandparents' understanding and support soothed weary men and women. Just talking about it helped.

During the discussion, one grandma told how she had spent that entire day in court and had come directly to this 7 p.m. meeting. Upon entering the courtroom that day for the hearing of a petition by her daughter for custody of her children, her daughter's attorney told Grandma to sit in the back, that she had nothing to contribute. Yet, during the proceeding, the judge responded to her raised hand when nobody else in the courtroom had the answers. Finally, the judge asked her to step forward and mildly rebuked her for sitting in the back. He carefully explained that in the state of Washington, she, the grandparent, had rights! Under the "Nonparental Custody Act," R.C.W. 26.10, she could petition the court for custody by proving that either:

• both parents were unsuitable or
• that the child was not in the custody of either parent.

This knowledge gave her new courage, which she brought to the support group meeting and which provided every grandparent there with new hope.

NONPARENTAL CUSTODY ACT

Michael W. Bugni (Bew'-nee), a Seattle attorney with experience in grandparenting custody cases, says,

Washington is one of the few states which has a "Parenting Act" i.e., resolving custody issues by means of a nonadversarial "Parenting Plan" instead of the traditional "custody" and "visitation rights" terminology. This law for "parents" resulted in a separate law being passed for third-party custody cases. In most cases, the "third party" will be a grandparent or a stepparent who seeks custody of, or visitation rights with, a nonbiological child. A "third party" custody or visitation case can also occur as the fallout from a divorce between the parents, in which case the grandparent would intervene as a party in the divorce action.

In order to be awarded custody, a grandparent is not required to prove that the parents are "unfit" in

107

the same sense that the state must prove a parent "unfit" to remove a child from that parent's home. Nevertheless, a grandparent must prove that leaving the child with the parent would be detrimental to the child's welfare. It would not be enough simply to show that the grandparent would do a better job of raising the child. That is to say that, all things being essentially equal, the Court will always award custody to a natural parent as opposed to anyone else. In a traditional custody case between two natural parents, the Court *does* weigh the relative strengths and weaknesses of the parents, and then awards custody to the "better" parent. The legal standard for a third-party custody, i.e., grandparent or stepparent, is somewhere between this "better parent" approach and the "must prove unfitness" approach. In my experience, the courts tend to overlook the technical case law, however, and simply do what they feel is best for the child. If a child has lived with his or her grandparents for a long time and if the child is doing well, a court will be reluctant to remove the child and return him or her to a natural parent. Grandparents must always give *both* parents notice of their intention to seek "custody" or "guardianship," even if it means publishing in the newspaper.[2]

GUARDIANSHIP AND CUSTODY

Many grandparents who have legal care of their grandchild actually did not obtain the child by filing *either* a "custody" or a "guardianship" case. Often the Child Protective Service has already removed the child from one or both of the natural parents; their policy is to then place the child (if possible) with a close family relative, usually a grandparent.

In that case, says attorney Bugni,

The Department of Social and Health Services main-
tains the ultimate control as to the child's placement.
They can unilaterally remove the child from the grandparents and even place the child in foster care if they
feel this would be best. This can and does happen
where the State has instructed the grandparents to
allow no contact (or supervised contact only) between child and parent and where a grandparent does
not comply. If the child remains with the grandparents for a long period of time under State placement,
however, eventually the State may encourage the
grandparents to seek legal custody of the child on
their own so that the State can then withdraw from
overseeing the child's placement. So long as the State's
case is pending in Juvenile Court, however, neither
the grandparents nor anyone else can pursue a separate "custody" or "guardianship" case in Superior
Court unless the Court specifically orders that the
two cases can proceed simultaneously. That is, a
State "dependency" case supersedes a private "custody" or "guardianship" case.[3]

Grandparents raising grandchildren without going
through legal channels are estimated to be in the thousands in America. These grandparents are just "helping
out" until a son or daughter gets his or her life in order,
which may never happen. In cases where the adult child's
circumstances change and the parent wants the child returned, the grandparents who are doing a good deed and
are legally unprotected, must give up the child and often
experience emotional calamity.

VISITATION

A grandparent's right to visit grandchildren seems undeniable. Yet images of the happy family—mother, father, and children—welcoming Grandma and Grandpa into their home, of excited youngsters bustling off to spend the weekend with grandparents, often do not mesh with life's realities.

Disputes involving minor children arise when a widowed son-in-law moves away from his children's maternal grandparents; when a former daughter-in-law remarries and her new husband adopts her children; when an unmarried mother refuses visitation to her child's paternal grandparents; or when a married son refuses to let his parents see their grandchildren. Conflict arises most often, however, during and after divorce.

Stephanie Edelstein is an associate director for the American Bar Association Commission on Legal Problems of the Elderly. In an article in *Modern Maturity,* Edelstein said,

> Every state has enacted some kind of legislation addressing grandparents' (visitation) rights. Here is a synopsis of how various states handle grandparents' rights of visitation:
>
> The majority of the states permit only grandparents to apply. But fully one-third (Alaska, Arizona, Arkansas, California, Connecticut, Hawaii, Illinois, Louisiana, Maine, Michigan, Nevada, New Jersey, North Dakota, Ohio, Utah, Washington, and Wisconsin) recognize that children may form close attachments to persons other than biological grandparents and allow siblings, great-grandparents, other relatives, and in some cases, non-relatives to seek visitation.
>
> Although state statutes provide the basic structure

in the area of grandparent visitation, they do not address every concern. The court must consider the evidence presented, apply the state's laws and, in most states, make a decision based on the "best interests" of the child.

In 1989 the American Bar Association adopted a policy encouraging mediation services in visitation cases and recommending that state legislation enumerate specific factors for courts to consider in determining whether grandparent visitation is in the child's best interests.[4]

LEGAL RIGHTS

Because the issue of grandparents raising grandchildren is still new and, state by state, new laws are being enacted, many grandparents do not know their legal rights. Attorneys interviewed for this book urged that grandparents create a legal basis for taking on this responsibility, regardless of the agreed upon time commitment with the child's parent or parents. You will find information on procedures in your local library reference department under Family Law, at your local bar association, from your state representative, or from an attorney.

Attorney Don J. Gough emphasizes that in the United States judicial system, no federal law exists pertaining to extended family or third-party custody; it is the exclusive province of the individual state. (You can request the FBI to investigate when a grandchild is taken across state lines.)

Gough says, "Although not always clearly defined, the 'best interest' of the child is always the language and the basis for decision in any state. Not who will do the best job or who will not, but what is in the best interest of the child."[5]

Seeking legal custody of grandchildren can be an expensive venture. In one case, grandparents spent three years and more than $100,000 trying to get custody of their two-year-old grandson and lost.

Legal custody to protect you and your grandchild from expected and unexpected happenings can cost from $750 up. Again, this is a new area for attorneys. It is important that you choose one who is compassionate, caring, and eager to help you find a smooth road to custody for the sake of your beloved grandchildren.

Legal custody is an explosive, many-sided issue. Emotions play a huge role in what happens. Sometimes what a grandparent wants for a grandchild is not in the child's best interest. A case in point is the custody battle between older grandparents and their daughter for two grandchildren:

Because of the daughter's drug addiction, the grandparents have cared for the children in their home for two years, during which time the grandparents and children have strongly bonded. The grandparents, focusing their lives on the children, have turned their home into a "child care center" filled with children's furniture and toys. The doting caregivers attempt to control every hour of their grandchildren's daily routine.

The daughter is now living with a man who has taken up her cause to bring the children back "home." Even though the daughter has not yet completed her drug therapy and is in a less than stable home environment, authorities and the drug therapist agree that leaving the children in the grandparents' home would be harmful to them because of the intensity of the grandparents' fight and their deluded perception of the situation.

According to the attorney who is attempting to mediate this volatile argument, "The grandparents have gone too far. They express only anger and hostility to their daughter and insist on custody while the mother and the authorities offer them visitation. Although there is fault on both sides here, the grandparents will not win the children because of the implacable attitude they bring to the fray. Time will tell how much damage their approach causes the children they love."

Before beginning the battle for legal custody of a grandchild, ask yourself this question:

"Do I want to do this because I have a *right* to or do I want to do this because, when I have examined all the circumstances, I know it is the most loving thing I can do for my grandchild?"

Having the legal right to petition for custody does not mean that it is necessarily the best approach to insuring a safe, secure future for a grandchild.

Putting first the goal of attaining what is in the best interest of the child is not only the way the legal authorities will evaluate the issue of custody, but it is always the most loving approach for a grandparent who wishes to have impact in a grandchild's life.

Let's examine our motives and attitudes carefully. How could the Lord want us to accomplish our good and honorable goals for our grandchildren?

The emotional distress of our kids can invade a grandparent's routine and well-being. How can a grandparent find sanity when it feels like the world is experiencing an invasion from another planet?

- Grown children casting about in a sea of discontent and bad decisions.
- Noisy children under foot.
- Well-intentioned children bungling the job.

In her devotional book, *Streams in the Desert*, Mrs. Charles E. Cowman gives us this life-preserving quote from Annie Johnson Flint: "All things move together for the purpose planned and behind the working is a mind CONTROLLING and a force DIRECTING, and a GUIDING HAND."

The Controller, the Director, the Guide is our loving Lord.

Jean Lush

9
...

Emotional Bankruptcy

What is a grandparent's role when their married children's lives are riddled with emotional turmoil, turmoil that affects the grandchildren?

OUR "MICROWAVE SOCIETY"

Young families today live in a "microwave society" with a mentality and technology that causes much stress. They have misplaced values where money and position are concerned, and work hard to "keep up" with inflated values. Relationships are stretched to the breaking point and healthy emotional wholeness is lost. What can we do?

First of all, you can hardly blame them for their emotional binds in this ungodly world where everyone wants everything instantly. During the winter of 1990, we watched a war, play by play, on television. Bombs were shot off thousands of miles away from a target; we watched them hit and instantly learned of the pain and loss of human life. Such immediacy invades our lives, sometimes desensitizing and distorting our view.

The impact of immediacy is reflected in our children. One of the first things we see in adult children experiencing emotional turmoil is unreached goals:

"I wanted to go to school this year, but we couldn't afford it."

"I don't have time to do the things I want to do."

"I don't want to work, but we need the money."

"I thought my husband would take care of me."

These young families are in desperate need of replacing the slippery slope with the rock foundation of the Word of God. If you have the privilege of influencing the direction of their lives, teach them to expect of themselves only what they can reasonably accomplish. "Humility and the fear of the Lord bring wealth and honor and life" (Prov. 22:4).

Teach them to take a fresh approach in relationship to each other and to the child(ren), relying on the Lord's strength and not their own. "Trust in the Lord with all your heart and lean not on your own understanding; in all your ways acknowledge him, and he will make your paths straight" (Prov. 3:5, 6).

Inspire them to wait on the Lord. Kids in this fast-paced society can learn that they have the ability to *wait*. "I wait for the Lord, my soul waits, and in his word I put my hope" (Ps. 130:5). Inspire them by your example. Be the calm sea in the storm.

Give them a guide to safe harbor. "God is our refuge and strength, an ever-present help in trouble" (Ps. 46:1).

MEDDLING

A fine line exists between healthy concern for our children's lives and meddling.

118

Meddling usually relates to control. *"If you ask me, I wouldn't do it that way!"* We break in without being invited.

Concern has a balance to it. *"How did you come to that conclusion?"* We see, hear, and comprehend.

We need to deal with the issues of the past in our own lives in order to respond to others' needs. Otherwise, we see our children's problems and issues through a dark glass, clouded with our own agenda.

Sad stories are told of young parents who refuse to bring children to see Grandma and Grandpa because of past meddling not yet resolved. Meddling brings down Mountain Time with grandchildren and everybody loses. Meddling is something you can control, something you can fix. You can admit it, accept forgiveness, then give it to the Lord in prayer and never do it again.

TAKING THEM IN

Should we take adult children and grandchildren back into our homes when they're in emotional chaos from divorce, abandonment, or abuse?

In Isaiah 25:4, the prophet praises the Lord: "You have been a refuge for the poor, a refuge for the needy in his distress, a shelter from the storm and a shade from the heat."

We can be a Christ-centered refuge for these children. Because of the world economy, the stress to make ends meet, and other conditions, it's tough for a single parent to live alone with children. It's hard enough to keep a job, let alone provide groceries, gas to and from work, childcare, and make the car payment. Little or none is left over to pay for extras. Sometimes the only option is to go home.

Jean Lush, counselor to parents for more than forty years, knows the pros and cons of kids returning home:

119

Grandparenting Redefined

"Many thousands of grandparents are giving up their cherished and orderly life-style, the fruit of hard work over a long period of time, to devote themselves and their earthly treasures to their grandchildren. I count it a priceless privilege to have had, even to this day, my grandchildren in and out of the house over our 54 year marriage. It has kept us young and watchful of our own Christian walk as we have opportunity to pass on to them our heritage. Difficulties come into play, however, when there are not clear guidelines set for behavior when kids come home to roost." [1]

As you accept these waifs into your safe haven, let them know at the outset that this is a transition time, a temporary arrangement for them to reorganize, stabilize, and formulate new goals. Make it clear that you want to be there for them, that you love them and want to provide emotional security *until* they can regroup and resume their lives.

Lush says, "When children and their children return home, grandparents face some things they never expected, never wanted and were not trained to handle. Behind this move may be heartbreaking reasons which make all three generations sad and distraught, wondering if God ever heard their earnest prayers. The most important thing for the grandparent to do is take the lead and find balance in a totally new and usually sad situation. This will mean the setting up of clear boundaries for everyone involved." [2]

Depending upon what the grandchild has endured, this can be a positive time of loving and affirming—a rewarding time of joy as you experience the "firsts" in a grandchild's life. Many years may have passed since your own child's growing up and, in a way, you can experience a grandchild's gleeful discoveries with more joy because they're new and fresh and bring back cherished memories.

"Coming back home" can result in great difficulties when the adult child is returning to the home in which he or she was raised. The house is filled with subtleties—the same old bedroom, the places of childhood play. It's easy to lapse into a comfort zone without boundaries. You risk enabling them to relate to you as childhood parent again but now parent of their whole family. By enabling the adult child to avoid taking responsibility for actions, goal setting, and emotional health, you enable failure and can end up frustrated, feeling intrusion into your life. The key here is to maintain an adult relationship with the adult child, not allowing the child to slip into complacency and dependency. Allow suffering of consequences of choices and actions.

Easy to say. Hard to do. Hold fast to John 12:24: "Unless a kernel of wheat falls into the ground and dies, it remains only a single seed. But if it dies, it produces many seeds."

As grandparents, we die to what we want. For a while.

HONORING THE CHOICES

Many of today's single parents refuse to return home with the kids, seeing such a move as further failure. They want to make it on their own and prove something. To return home to the place where they grew up is an unthinkable option. We need to understand that decision, honor it, and nurture that independence.

Conversely, we need to honor the decision to bring this beloved package of raw emotion back into the home by

• making clear and steadfast rules;

• sticking to the rules—no matter what happens;

• making way for growth and the taking of responsibility for your grandchildren.

Adult kids in emotional trouble need a shoulder to cry on. They need a listener, someone who will take it all in, with compassion and understanding, someone who will not judge them but accept their feelings and fears until they themselves hear what they are saying and can begin to see a path toward resolution or reconciliation.

Adult kids in emotional trouble need discipline; not reprimand and reproof but a sense of order, a clear approach to a new beginning. It is only as we put away our own prejudices and pre-conceived ideas that we can begin to be God's instrument for growth and change.

A grandparent's heart is patient, never giving up on a grandchild's potential and future. A child who is far from the Lord touches a grandparent's heart in profound ways.

The grandparent who is willing to forgive at the slightest indication of repentance ... willing to listen and offer help and counsel ... is a unique tool in the hands of our God to nurture, guide, and love that grandchild back to him.

David Hocking

10

...

Spiritual Bankruptcy

What is a grandparent's role when grandchildren walk away from their faith or are not in a home where their faith is nurtured?

Jacqueline McCoy, a respected Christian counselor with CRISTA Counseling Service in Seattle, has helped many grandparents and other family members through difficult times. She says: "A grandparent is no different from a parent or anyone else when it comes to advising or nurturing a child who has walked away from the Lord. Before you can be of any help to that grandchild, you must first deal with your own 'stuff.' When you feel angry or upset that your grandchild is no longer attending church, is not being nurtured in his or her faith, or has reached teen years and is rebelling, you need to examine whether your feelings are your own honest reactions or 'righteous indignation.' You may be feeling out of control of this child who is not walking with the Lord. You want to look like a good grandparent who's done everything right. So—look at yourself and your motives. Is your frustration based upon your need to feel good about yourself? Are you just worried about what people will think?

"If that's the case, come to grips with it. Your life is not in that child. Your life is in Jesus Christ and he is the one who validates your existence. Not what you or your grandchildren do but what Christ has done for you by his death on the cross, his all-sufficient grace, and his restoration power. As long as we are looking to our grandchildren to get our needs met for wholeness, acceptance, and love, we are going to be disappointed. We need to remind ourselves of what is true in terms of eternal life and act upon that instead of from what people are going to think or say." [1]

LOVING CONFRONTATION

McCoy reminds us that before we can say anything to a grandchild about walking with the Lord, we must first diffuse anxiety so as not to get our own "stuff" mixed up in it. Then a conversation can begin with an "I" statement:

• "I'm concerned that you're not attending church anymore."
• "I have some concerns I'd like to share with you."

Don't use accusatory "you" statements:

• "You're not going to church anymore!"
• "You'd better get your spiritual life in order!"

A good approach would be, "I've noticed you (and your mom and dad) are not attending church, and I'm concerned about you since that has always been important to me. Do you feel like talking about it?" Speaking from your own experience is nonthreatening and harder to refute. "I've had the most problems in my life at those times I wasn't attending church." This kind of loving confrontation points out truths by example and in a way that continues to affirm and show care, not rejection because of what has happened.

I believe this is what brings people back to the Lord. Not "ragging" them about their spiritual life but loving them and showing yourself as a Christ-like example. Leave the rest to the Holy Spirit.

Pray for your grandchildren daily. It is hard to accept that you can't affect your adult children's lives to the extent you could when they were growing up and that now, you need to let go. You no longer have control over their lives or, certainly, the lives of your grandchildren. Praying for grandchildren is probably the best thing you can do.

TEACH LIKE A PARENT

We've lost control. But as grandparents, we might be in an even better position to teach our grandchildren because we have more emotional distance than the parent. We might be more objective, which could lead to more openness in the relationship. Let the children see that you go to church, pray, and reverence the Lord. Talk about your faith with grandchildren. They'll pick up on it as important and somewhere along the line may incorporate your values into their own lives.

KEEP JESUS BEFORE THEM

Storybooks about the Lord are effective teaching tools when the children visit you. Amy Grant has a Bible storybook with questions at the end of each page. Kids learn to relate to positive moral values as they think for themselves.

The "McGee and Me" video series is a valuable tape to watch with grandchildren. And for Christmas, a video entitled "The Troll Prince" communicates a clear metaphor for Christ coming into the world.

Use cut-and-paste projects for bad-weather times. Jacqueline McCoy is also a grandmother and tells of a special time with her grandchildren who call her "Nana."

"We got dressed up for church and couldn't get there because of a bad snowstorm. So we sang songs, read a Bible story, and played hymns on the piano. Then we worked together on making paper snowflakes. I explained that just as each snowflake is different, so God has made each one of us different—beautiful and special in our own way. We cut out the snowflakes and taped them to the kitchen door. After that, the kids wanted to have Sunday school at Nana's house every time." [2]

When grandchildren stay overnight on Saturday, take them with you to church on Sunday morning. Say grace at the table. Better yet, ask them to say it. Speak from your personal perspective about the Lord and share the excitement about the great things he is doing in your life. One of them, of course, is that he gave you your precious grandchildren!

Be aware of opportunities. Get your licks in when you can.

SHATTERED IMAGES

Sometimes, it is through the heinous sin of sexual abuse that our grandchildren lose their faith.

Fourteen-year-old Carrie's father, a deacon in the church, sexually abused her for seven years before she found help. Carrie said, "Every night I'd go to bed and pray Jesus would help me, protect me, and keep my dad away from me. And every morning, early, he would come into my room."

This young woman will have a difficult time relating to God as protector, a person who will not take advantage of her the way her father did. Children look upon their parents as their "image" of God—their "example" of God. The sin of incest has so damaged her ability to relate to God that it will take many years to bring her to a right spirit.

As grandparents, we can claim for Carrie the promise of Scripture in Joel 2:24-27, "I am the Lord your God and there is no other; never again will my people be shamed." Almighty God will make up for the "locust" of parental abuse. As he made up for the years that locusts devoured the crops of Judah, so he will refresh and renew the barrenness of an innocent child's soul. He alone can erase the bitterness and resentment and gently, lovingly, as a father should, bring her back to a life of faith.

The sin of emotional abuse is no less abhorant than sexual or physical abuse. Grandchildren might stop believing in God when they are called a liar, for example, by a parent or grandparent—an authority figure in their lives. Calling children a liar labels them, gives them a name other than their own. Emotional abuse cuts to the quick of a little person's integrity, sometimes for a lifetime.

A better response to a child's dishonesty might be, "I'm disappointed when you lie," or "We don't like lying here." This way, we speak to the behavior and not the person.

Again, children, especially young children, see their parents as "God-like" people in their lives. Until they are able to see God as bigger than their parents, their concept of God is filtered through the lens of what they experience with their parents. If it is rejection, criticism, abandonment, abuse, inconsistency, or punishment, they'll view God the same way.

"Does God really love me?"

"How can God love me if my mommy (or daddy) doesn't?"

A grandparent can be a loving, consistent stabilizer for a grandchild whose own parents are not acting in a loving manner and can bring some balance and normalcy to the child's life.

We have our grandchildren for such a little while. Too soon they become adults.

No matter where they live, down the street or across the country, no boundary line can stop the flow of love to them from Grandma and Grandpa. Be mindful of every opportunity to teach them, by word and deed, about our Lord and his sovereignty in their lives.

Not a moment should be wasted. They need us as much as we need them.

Lillian Iverson

11

...

Grandchildren Far Away

When a grandchild moves away because of divorce, remarriage, or worse, how can a grandparent maintain a relationship with that child? It is possible. And it can be fun. All it takes is a little planning and a lot of love. Even if separated by a half-century and a whole continent, you and your grandchild can be best friends.

TELEPHONE TECHNIQUES

Try a Sunday morning phone call before church. Then go and pray for your grandchild. Hearing that familiar voice will hold you for the rest of the week.

Make more than small talk. Build on past discussions. Talk about school projects, upcoming recitals, and sporting events. "If you share a mutual hobby or sport such as fishing, skiing, or stamp collecting, you won't walk into conversations cold," says Dr. Barry Smith, a pediatrician

Grandparenting Redefined

in El Cajon, California.[1]

Know what's going on in your grandchild's life. What is his or her favorite TV program? Watch it once, then call and discuss it. Which of the Teenage Mutant Ninja Turtles, for example, does your grandchild like best? Why? As your grandchild grows, make phone calls special times to talk about both of your lives. Tell how you spent Saturday morning watching a blue jay feed her nest of babies outside your window. Such word pictures let the child in on a significant part of your life.

Talking about mutual interests and pertinent details of a grandchild's life is far more effective than, for example: "Hi! How are you doin'? What's going on? What do ya' mean, nothing?"

Have patience with young children, for it takes them a little longer and you will receive only brief replies. Your strategic silences will show you are really listening.

It also takes patience to telephone teenagers. All I get sometimes is a "Yup" or a "Nope." That's okay. I understand.

WRITING STORIES

Mike Moldeven's grandkids live far away. This energetic seventy-two-year-old retired military analyst lives in California and decided one day that phone visits with his Portland grandchildren weren't enough.

He created story ideas when he was with his grandkids, and then followed them up with a written "tailored" tale to send them in the mail. He focused most of his stories on their shared good times, interwoven with subtle lessons on morality and goodness. He based all of his stories on his own experiences with his grandchildren. After mailing off some twenty-five stories to the delight of the recipients, Moldeven gathered his stories into a self-published book,

Write Stories to Me, Grandpa!

"Anybody can do what I've done," he says. "If you can't write, you can tape stories using your own voice on a tape recorder. It's a wonderful way to pass along family traditions, awareness, and values and a great way to keep in touch."[2]

TEACHING LONG DISTANCE

Grandson Joshua, age six, lives two thousand miles away from his grandma and grandpa. Here is how Grandma Iverson says they keep in touch:

"Joshua goes to a Christian school in Chicago. We have much in common because I taught at a Christian school in Seattle for many years. So we talk by phone about what he's learning, what he's made, and how he's acted out Bible stories in special plays.

"I listen carefully and answer carefully, especially when Joshua has a question about the Lord.

"I write poems for his birthday, Christmas, Thanksgiving, Easter, and Valentine's Day. I send the 'funnies' from the Sunday paper and add my own words in the spaces.

"I write Joshua about the possums that sneak by our back windows, the squirrels that stash their winter food under the tree stump, the raccoons that thump onto our roof, and how sweetly the birds at our bird feeders trill their thanks to God.

"Sometimes I adapt Bible stories so he can better understand God's lessons. I teach him the poems I learned as a girl, which he in turn teaches his little sister, Shannon, age three. I challenge Joshua to memorize Scripture. He sings and makes up his own songs, like this one:

"Jesus loves me so much.
He loves me when I am good and
he loves me when I'm bad.

135

And why does he love me so much?
Just because." [3]

Just because. All of his life, Joshua will remember that he can come to Jesus and receive unconditional love.

We don't have to live next door to our grandchildren to teach them Christian values and practical everyday helps.

THE STORY VIDEO

Remember that a picture can be worth a thousand phone calls. "For many children under eight or nine, phone conversations are difficult," says Dr. David Elkind, author of *Grandparenting: Understanding Today's Children*. If you have access to a camcorder, Elkind suggests making a video of yourself talking or singing to your grandchild or giving a guided tour of your home and neighborhood.[4]

Another good idea for video is Grandma and/or Grandpa reading a bedtime story to a little grandchild. Read it out of a storybook and send the book along so the child can turn the pages and look at the pictures. Tell stories of family history and what you did at your grandchild's age or even make up stories about imaginary characters.

"You won't have to spend most of your waking hours recording stories to meet the need for a nightly tale," says Miriam Galper Cohen, family therapist and author of *Long-Distance Parenting*, "because young children love repetition and will be glad to hear the same story over and over again."[5] The child's parents can use the tape at bedtime, discuss it, and then pray for you. Ask them to videotape that exchange for you, as well!

THE ART OF LETTER WRITING

Write your grandchild regularly, maybe every two weeks or so, and encourage a written response. Print for the young ones. Enclose colorful paper, envelopes, and stamps.

An occasional dollar bill, sticker, or riddle adds to the fun.

That way, both generations will look forward to visits from the mailman. According to George Newman, coauthor of *The Grandparenting Book*, children love getting mail addressed to them, even if they can't read it themselves. It makes them feel important. By including magazine clippings about other youngsters their age, animals, funny tales, or sports, you might help the child's reading skills without it seeming like homework. Selecting unusual stamps for the envelope might encourage an interest in stamp collecting.

SENDING GIFTS

Keep gifts small and inexpensive. A dollar bill for small children and maybe ten dollars for a teen. A Bible marker with a scripture quotation or stickers. The important thing is the love the gift represents.

Note cards and envelopes, stamps, cassette tapes, and videotapes are all gifts that will return to you and perpetuate the exchange of love, caring, and tradition.

Family therapist Cohen says, "It's important to establish yourself as a presence in the hearts and minds of your grandchildren. Instill yourself—your history—your values—in your grandkids. But most of all, have fun with them. They'll be grown up before you know it!" [6]

Through his Word, God has dictated responsibility. He has said he will take care of our needs. He has said he will provide even for the bird in the field.

However, it is not God who places the worm in the young bird's open mouth. He gives the bird a beak, wings to fly, and feet to dig out the worm. And he gives responsibility in the process—responsibility even a bird cannot shirk.

In Proverbs 13:22, God tells us, "A good man leaves an inheritance for his children's children." Our inheritance to our grandchildren is truly blessed when it is preceded by and built upon God's wisdom and his biblical principles.

David Bragonier

12

...

Grandparents and Money

The couple looked like ideal prospects for the new retirement center where I was employed on the marketing staff. Both were in their late sixties, he with a plaid tam at a cocky slant on his head, she dressed in bright-colored casual clothes. As they entered the office with a lively stride, he announced, "We're the McTavishes. Just here to look around. Come along, Peg!"

Brushing by my outstretched hand, they stepped into the model unit. Obviously, Mr. McTavish knew where he wanted to go and what he wanted to see. Mrs. McTavish, however, could not see enough.

She looked up at the ceilings, down at the floors, and stroked the dining room table as if she hadn't ever seen one so lovely. As they made their way to a bedroom, which had been decorated for display as a den, I heard Mrs. McTavish whisper to her husband, "Oh, John, this is what I've always wanted for you . . . a study where you can put your books and have a place to—"

"Hush now, girl!" he stopped her in his thick Scottish brogue. "We'll have none of that! I only came by this place because you insisted. We've seen it. Let's go!"

"But John . . ." His wife struggled to hold back tears and tugged at his arm as he tried to leave the room. "This is where we said we'd spend our retirement years, in this beautiful Christian center where our friends will live. This is what you have worked so hard for all these years!" Her small frame began to shake gently.

"Now, girl . . ." He placed his hands on her shoulders and drew her to him. "There's no way we can do that now. That was just a dream we had. We have to let it go. Come on now, sit over here for a spell and then we'll be on our way."

Waiting a few courteous minutes, I walked into the model living room and swallowed hard. "Well, Mr. and Mrs. McTavish, are there any questions I can answer for you?"

Peg hid the last tear and smiled a smile that held no joy. A smile that said, "Oh, yes, but what's the use?"

John, still with an arm around his wife, looked squarely at me. "Young lady, there was a time when we'd have plenty of questions for ya', and we'd be givin' the answers that would be pleasin' to ya', but not anymore. There's no way we can move in here. Our grandkids got all our money!"

Over the next half-hour, John and Peg McTavish told me about their son and daughter-in-law and the twin grand-daughters.

She said, "They're just wonderful grandchildren! We'd do anything for them!"

And they had. Piano lessons. Trips. College. Cars. Clothes.

"We were making an investment in our grandchildren, ya' see," said Grandpa McTavish.

It seemed clear that the twins' parents had allowed, if not encouraged, this investment with no monetary return, and now these generous grandparents needed their money back. Some promissory notes had been signed for college and car expenses but had lapsed unpaid. It would be years before they could pay any of it back. Years from now would be too late. These grandparents had depleted their savings and IRA and were left with a house to sell and his pension from forty years in the tool-and-die business. Without a better financial statement, it was doubtful they could move into a retirement center.

Even though this is an extreme example of grand-parenting generosity, what can we learn from it?

In 1 Timothy 5:8, Paul admonishes, "If anyone does not provide for his relatives, and especially for his immediate family, he has denied the faith and is worse than an unbeliever."

What does that mean to a grandparent? How much do we give of our earthly treasure to our children for the well-being of our grandchildren? Do we give it freely to grandchildren or do we expect to get it back? When should we give and when should we not?

THE SACRAMENTS OF LENDING

Financial counselor Larry Burkett says in *Using Your Money Wisely*, "There's an old saying that the definition of a distant friend is a close friend who owes you money." [1]

You can probably double the distance if the borrower is a relative.

David Bragonier, an area coordinator for Larry Burkett and director of Barnabas, Inc., a Christian financial training ministry, advises grandparents to use discernment before becoming financially involved with grandchildren, or with any member of their family: "A grandparent must make sure to set a godly and scripturally-based example." [2]

Bragonier recommends the following considerations when addressing difficult and emotional monetary decisions relating to our grandchildren:

Prayer

Whether the need is expressed to you or you observe it yourself, pray before taking action. Ask God, "Am I the person to take care of this need?" God may want to do something else in the situation. Take time to discern his will.

Planning

Grandparents should have a written financial plan, including projected income and expenses for the next twelve months and long-term goals, such as retiring at a special retirement center. God's Word makes it clear we are to make plans. Planning brings balance and responsibility into our lives and sets an example for grandchildren to follow.

Most grandparents desire to help their grandchildren financially. However, as in the story at the beginning of this chapter, emotions enter into this desire. When grandparents' goals are written out and expenses recorded, it's easier to set aside emotion and make a balanced decision. Planning moves emotions off the table so all the facts get on the table. After planning, if we choose to help our grandchildren, it is with the knowledge that we may have to give up reaching one of our own important and necessary goals.

Authority

Grandparents must not usurp the authority of their grandchild's parents. The Bible admonishes the man to "leave" his father and mother and "cleave" to his wife. The two of them now become one flesh. Our children and their children become their own family unit. This is not to say that the new family should exclude the grandparents. Hopefully, everyone enjoys a relationship with one another. But once our children marry, the authority structure changes.

The grandparents are now a source of counsel to this new family; that counsel must be requested by them and not forced upon them. If our children understand the wisdom God has given to us as parents, they will eagerly seek our counsel.

If a grandchild does seek our counsel, we must know that they first sought the counsel of their parents and what counsel was given. If ours differs, we can talk with the parents before counseling the grandchild further. We don't want to undermine the parents' authority by failing to consult with them about our financial plans for our grandchildren.

Communication

Unclear communication and unexpressed expectations cause most of the financial stress between family members. Loving grandparents tend to say, "Oh, don't worry about the money. We'll figure out the details later." We must be willing to jeopardize our relationship with our grandchildren, if necessary, to clearly communicate our intentions and expectations. If money is loaned, write out the exact terms and conditions of the loan, including what will happen if the money is not paid back.

Responsibility

Obviously, we are not talking about every little gift we give a grandchild. But when substantial amounts of money leave our hands, it is up to us grandparents to teach grandchildren responsibility. Conversely, we can examine our motives in gifting or loaning money by asking:

Grandparenting Redefined

"Am I meeting my grandchild's need or my own need to give?"

"Why does the child have this need? Is it irresponsibility, slothfulness, indulgence, or greed?"

"Can my grandchild obtain this another way and learn more responsibility?"

"By giving or lending this money, will I become a stumbling block to an understanding of stewardship?"

Again, we are not talking about every little decision. If grandparents want to pay for piano lessons and the parents feel good about it, then the grandparents must only decide whether or not they can personally afford the lessons. And the grandchildren must understand that this does not set a precedent for all financial decisions.

Accountability

If we are giving or loaning money because of an unmet need due to irresponsibility, then accountability should be a part of the gift or loan. Third-party financial counseling and accountability might be needed and required as a condition of the gift or loan.

Scriptural Wisdom

The Bible does not say we cannot loan money to friends and relatives. However, the Bible does say: "The rich rule over the poor and the borrower is servant to the lender" (Prov. 22:7). Any time we loan money to anyone, for any reason, our relationship with that person changes because of this principle. Even if the grandparent is not concerned about pay back, the borrower still feels some servitude because of the borrower–lender relationship.

We can always choose to forgive the loan, which under certain circumstances, might be a valuable lesson to the grandchild. Also, sometimes it would be better for everyone involved to find another source for the money or, instead of loaning it, simply give it. But even in gifting, we must consider the above cautions.

GIFTING

The process of gifting and expecting nothing in return is made easier if we trained up our children, their parents, to be good stewards of money. If we did, we can share a mutual understanding with the parents as to our motivation and desired goals for giving. For example, it is tough today for young families to purchase a first home. Parents and grandparents working creatively to make this a reality for your grandchild can be a satisfying and memorable time for all. I know one set of grandparents who, with the parents' approval, co-purchased a home with the grandchild, paying one-half of the monthly mortgage. Later, when the grandchild's earning capacity was greater, he assumed the grandparents' portion of the mortgage, releasing them from further obligation.

If we neglected to train our children to handle money wisely, and if we don't consult with them as parents, we face being misunderstood and even used, as seemed to be the case with the McTavishes.

To Give Or Not To Give

Following are five reasons Bragonier suggests avoiding monetary gift-giving at a particular time.

1. If your motivation is guilt about something that happened or didn't happen in the past.

2. If the gift-giving process doesn't teach the child something about God and his biblical principles.

3. If the child is outwardly rebellious against God. (Remember, however, that if the child is a good person who simply has not yet accepted the Lord, your gift might

147

be the instrument to draw him or her to eternal salvation.)

4. If you don't have it to give. Assess your own capabilities. Placing an undue burden on yourself to answer a grandchild's need is negative motivation, which can lead to serious consequences. We don't have to be "the dollar." We can be "the process" toward fulfillment of the goal.

5. If you are indulging them. What is your gift teaching your grandchild about hard work and reward? As grandparents, we must be willing to allow grandchildren to suffer in order for God to bring about the changes he wants in their lives.[3]

GIFTING VERSUS INHERITANCE

What are the positives and negatives of giving while still alive versus leaving an inheritance to grandchildren?

Scripture tells us in 1 Timothy 6:7: "For we brought nothing into the world, and we can take nothing out of it." Even with that reality, assigning to grandchildren or anyone else what the Lord has temporarily entrusted to us before *or* after our death is a personal and individual decision.

Some grandparents receive great satisfaction from watching the progress a grandchild makes because of their gift. Others prefer to trust the money to a third party, a trustee, who monitors changes in the child's life, whether or not the grandparent is alive. Some refuse to give if the grandchild is living in open disobedience to God's laws and others wish to name the grandchildren in a will.

Attorney Lyle K. Wilson specializes in estate planning. He reminds us that a couple can give away up to twenty thousand dollars per year to as many people as they wish, tax free, but that grandparents should ask themselves:

Will this gift have an adverse impact on the child's

own incentive to make a way in this world? Will it create the expectation that he or she needn't be creative and resourceful, that good old Grandpa and Grandma will bail them out from the DWI, the traffic tickets, the overdue rent? And if a grandparent is giving big money and decides to pull the plug, cut the grandchild off for irresponsibility or whatever, things can become ugly. In one case, a grandmother doled out money by the tens of thousands to a grandson. When his business failed, she would set him back on his feet so he could fail again. On my recommendation, she cut him off. The grandson responded by standing in her yard, screaming obscenities and curses at her. It's difficult to turn the spigot off. Once you start down that road, you have created expectations and may find yourself giving up funds you need.[4]

Whether gifting while we're still here or naming a grandchild in a will, an important question is "As I give this gift, am I investing in the temporal or the eternal welfare of my grandchild?"

Remember the McTavishes? John and Peg finally told their son and daughter-in-law of their financial condition and their unfulfilled hope, which turned out to be shocking revelations to the adult son. He had assumed through the years that Mom and Dad wanted to help and were capable of giving to the children or they would not have done so. Although long overdue, this open communication led to resolution of the problems. The son and daughter-in-law had the money and paid all entrance costs for Grandma and Grandpa to move into the retirement center of their dreams. All parties met together with the twin granddaughters, who are now repaying their college debts and auto loans to their parents in honor of their grandparents.

PREPARING TO SURVIVE

Nursing homes in America are called sororities for good reason. More than seventy-five percent of their residents are women. In 1989, half of all older American women were widows, and there were five times as many widows (8.3 million) as widowers (1.7 million).[5] All of this means Grandma is probably going to outlive Grandpa!

Lawyers and financial counselors say that their saddest interviews are with older married women who were financially unprepared for widowhood. Many sail through the parenting season, mid-life, and into old age, completely dependent upon their husbands to take care of food, clothing, shelter, and future needs. For whatever reason, they are ill-prepared to lead a reasonably successful and secure life—alone.

Attorney Wilson suggests these important pointers prior to such an eventuality:

1. *Husband and wife should sit down together early to discuss financial arrangements for retirement.* The younger you are, the less long-term care or life insurance costs. Such a conversation can be emotional and even threatening, but you need to do it.

2. *Create a will or living trust arrangement, which provides for orderly disposition of the estate.* This is foundational and should be a priority even for young couples. Without a plan, disposition will be different from what was intended. In one case, a couple in a second marriage was living in a home owned by the wife before the marriage. She had died without a will and under the laws of that state, her children from the first marriage were entitled to half of her estate, including half of the house. Instead of her husband staying on in the house, it had to be sold and the funds divided, which caused a great deal of

anger between the stepchildren and the widower. Do not resort to mail order forms for important documents such as a will or living trust. See a competent, experienced attorney.

3. *Update the will or living trust as changes occur.*

4. *Be familiar with all bank accounts, bank locations, account numbers, balances and, if possible, the name of a contact at each one.*

5. *Understand all stock certificates and bonds owned.*

6. *Know your insurance agent's name and telephone number plus the amounts and stipulations of each policy.*

7. *Consider having a Living Will/Directive to Physicians/Durable Power of Attorney.* These inexpensive documents can save a lot of grief. Again, obtain the services of a competent attorney to help you. One woman, whose husband was in a nursing home, went to a bookstore for what she thought was a form for Durable Power of Attorney. It was in reality a "Special" Durable Power of Attorney with a big blank space in the middle to be filled out with specifics. The husband and wife signed the form, even had it notarized without filling out the specifics in the blank space. It said nothing and was invalid. Bookstore forms do not cover what needs to be covered. If you buy one, take it to an attorney.

8. *Make funeral arrangements ahead of time, especially if you know of special desires.*

9. *Keep all important papers in one place and easily accessible.*

10. *Do not presume you will go first.* You may never see bus loads of little old men, but we can't pre-suppose the wife will survive the husband or vice versa. Never plan around one or the other. Take care of both of you![6]

It is so easy to say, "I know just how you feel." But unless we have lost a child or grandchild, we cannot fathom the depth of grief that grabs onto the human heart when the word is given, "Your child is going to die."

I heard those words twice in two years as one son after another was born with fatal brain damage. I begged for some thread of hope but the doctor said, "This is something your money and your willpower can't do anything about." He was right.

In that double loss and later the premature death of a grandchild, I learned there are many things in life I can't do anything about. It was through these lessons that I accepted the Lord, the only One who can give peace in adverse circumstances.

"Weeping may remain for a night but rejoicing comes in the morning" (Ps. 30:5).

Florence Littauer

13
...

Grandchildren
Lost and Found

Grandparents who are sacrificing for their grandchildren are blessed to *have* their grandchildren. Whatever is going on in their lives that seems so catastrophic, so unmanageable, so hard to accept, *nothing* compares to the loss of a grandchild, the light of your grandparenting life.

Many grandparents make the ultimate sacrifice, giving up their grandchild to God's divine plan. Other grandparents know that some day they'll have to.

St. Patrick's Day, March 17, 1984. Grandma Mickey barely heard the phone.

"Mom?"

"Oh, hi, Honey! I was just vacuuming . . ."

"It's Kyle . . . he's in the hospital, Mom. They don't think they can revive him!"

The light of Mickey's life, twenty-month-old grandson Kyle, had fallen into a ditch near his home while playing.

155

Rain had filled the ditch and Kyle's mother found her little son lying in three feet of water.

Mickey darted through traffic to the hospital, overcome with terror. For five hours, the staff tried to revive Kyle to no avail. It was time to turn off the machines.

Dazed family members circled the little bed. In disbelief, Mickey silently screamed her thoughts. "This is not happening! The enemy is not going to get away with this! I am a Christian!"

She felt her mental capabilities drain away as they pulled the plug, gently wrapped the baby in a blanket and passed him, one by one, to each person. When her turn came to hold him, she noticed his little foot sticking out, the foot that showed the birthmark about the size of a nickel. Like a good grandma, Mickey quickly covered it against the air of the room, at the same instant realizing there was no need to do so. Grandma Mickey was numb, frozen in place as her distraught son urged her to hand Kyle to him. She had to let him go. She had to say goodbye to this little blonde bundle of joy who was just now learning his ABC's, who the other day had played with his car on the sidewalk, the car his grandma had given him . . . wearing his little lime green jacket.

Numbness persisted through the funeral arrangements. Mickey received the flowers of condolence, made the telephone calls to relatives, fixed the meals, answered the inquiries.

How could she burden the daughter she loved so much with any more pain by baring her own feelings? No. She had to be strong.

Her beloved grandson was laid to rest in the colorful quilt his grandma had made for him with the matching soft pillow under his head.

Mickey didn't buckle at the graveside service. How

could she? Someone had to row the boat!

Her son-in-law's business took him and her daughter out of town right after the funeral. They asked Mickey to visit the gravesite every day for the three weeks they would be gone. She went every day, bringing flowers and balloons—telling Kyle all the recent family news and how much everyone missed him.

She told him it was a beautiful day. A perfect day for a small boy in a little green coat to push his car, to run and laugh and play.

She told him, "I hate this day!"

The balloons said "Jesus Loves You," and Mickey sang "Jesus Loves You" to Kyle over and over again, day after day.

But inside, under the facade of strength, were smouldering questions and confusion.

"Is this a dream? Is this happening to me? This is not my pain! Let me go home and find all of my family there so I can share what I did for someone else today!"

To God she shouted, "Don't talk to me! I don't ever want to talk to you again!"

Mickey lived in secret rejection of God as she continued to go to church, keeping her feelings bottled up inside. No one knew. Her Christian friends came to wrap their arms around her in an attempt to share her pain. They called, sent cards and letters. She took it all in, hiding her sorrow.

One day a card arrived from Kyle's mother, who had been suffering deep grief at the loss of her son. She wrote: "God put a song in my heart today. . . . Joy is the flag that is flown from the castles of my heart when the King is in residence there. It felt so good to sing and to actually feel joy!"

Jesus reached out to soothe Mickey's soul as she read the words of joy from a mother's heart. She began to feel, really feel, the love so freely given by her family and friends, love that never let up. Unconditional love.

It was the beginning of Mickey's healing. Once again, she began to talk to God, to pray the prayers of thanksgiving as she had before. She spent hours praising God for providing the safety net of family and friends during this time of tragedy. He revealed to her that the Comforter had always been there, working through the deeds of his people. Once again, Mickey had the will to live.

Mickey was on the road to recovery but knew that if she were to find her way back to complete restoration, she needed to make a conscious decision to be totally well. "I don't want to be crippled any more!" she said.

But when the new youth pastor at her church came by to ask Mickey to head up a group at the church, a young people's drama team, she said, "No! No! I can't work with children! No!" She still could not look at a child without recalling her lost love.

The young man insisted Mickey come to the first meeting and decide for herself. Mickey finally agreed and was introduced to twenty-four endearing youngsters with whom she bonded immediately. For the past year, Mickey has enjoyed the love of her flock of twenty-four gifts from God.

On March 17, 1991, the seventh anniversary of Kyle's death, Mickey had a barbecue for her drama troupe. The kids brought her flowers and a card. Each one signed the card, "I love you." The last remnants of a grandmother's grief became a patchwork sewn together by the hand of God.

"I'm not completely there yet, but I understand so much more now! Some of my friends have experienced loss and didn't have the chance to say good-bye. I did! I got to hold Kyle and tell him one last time that his grandma loved him. That was a privilege some don't have. After I began to see through my tears and chose to heal, God bestowed this gift upon me—this chance to love, teach, and pray for twenty-four other youngsters. At long last, I've been made stronger at the broken place." [1]

ORPHANS OF AIDS

Babies are falling through the cracks in America's health care system—babies with AIDS. The parents' sins or their accidental acquisition of AIDS are wreaking terminal havoc on the innocents as parents die, are unable to care for, or walk away from the responsibility of their children.

Janet Trinkaus is founder and executive director of Rise 'n Shine, an organization in Seattle created to help victimized children. She says grandparents can play an important role in helping children cope with the fallout from AIDS.

"These kids didn't ask for the terrible predicament they are in. Some do not even have the virus but their parent does or the parent had it and perhaps has died, leaving them alone. Some kids are born with the virus or with full-blown AIDS acquired from their mothers during pregnancy. These kids become orphans of AIDS and desperately need someone who cares. When no family member comes forward to help, they go into foster homes. Our goal at Rise 'n Shine is to give these kids:

• unconditional love and joy
• self-esteem and dignity
• understanding and the opportunity to freely express feelings and emotions
• help in making choices
• one-on-one support relationships apart from those of their parents or caretakers

"We could use some loving grandparents to help out." [2]

Most major cities have organizations like Rise 'n Shine.

Grandparenting Redefined

Maybe you can volunteer some time and love for a needy child. Grandpa Ed took the challenge and has never regretted it. He reached out to help his own granddaughter.

Ed, a sixty-eight-year-old widower, knew his pregnant daughter, Andrea, had contracted the HIV virus. His worst fear came true when his granddaughter, sweet little Teresa, came into this world with full-blown AIDS. Teresa, just born, was going to die.

After a few months, Grandpa Ed moved in with Andrea and helped care for Teresa, physically and emotionally. While Andrea was at work, Grandpa Ed fed and bathed the baby, played with her, gave her necessary medications, sang to her, and held her hour after hour when she cried out. He took her in the stroller on sunny days so every passerby could see how beautiful she was. Teresa was developmentally delayed but a more cheerful child never lived! She smiled at everyone and showed remarkable curiosity about new things and new people.

One day, Andrea took Teresa on a short trip to see relatives who had never met her and she got sick. Later, at the hospital, doctors said she had pneumonia. Grandpa Ed knew Teresa would not come home again.

At two years, six months and three days of age, Teresa died. The innocent victim of AIDS.

Grandpa stays on with his daughter to this day. They are a comfort to each other. No one knows whether or not Andrea will develop AIDS; the virus lurks in her body. But Grandpa Ed knows he did his best to give his granddaughter a glimpse of life and to give his daughter the support and hope she needed during Teresa's lifetime.

Why did he do it?

"I love my daughter," he said tearfully. "And I adored my granddaughter. Teresa was the most beautiful little girl in the world. She gave me so much more than I gave her.

She made me feel valuable. God gave her such a zest for life. She was interested in everything. And God gave me two and a half years of the happiest memories a grandpa could ever have." [3]

SUDDEN INFANT DEATH SYNDROME

Every year as many as seven thousand babies die before their first birthday from Sudden Infant Death Syndrome (SIDS), the baffling "crib death" of infants. It is said that the death of a baby touches at least one hundred people, including grandparents.

Vera was one such grandparent. Grandmother of four bouncing boys, she had waited patiently for a granddaughter. When Antonia finally arrived, she became the apple of her grandmother's eye. Named for her Dutch aunt, beautiful, healthy Antonia brought much happiness into Vera's son and daughter-in-law's home and to many others.

One morning her parents, hearing nothing from the baby's room, wondered why she wasn't yet awake. Walking into the room, mother Janie screamed. The baby was in her crib, face down and blue. Antonia's daddy, Gary, began sobbing unconsolably, crying out, "If only I'd . . . If only I. . . ."

The ambulance driver comforted Gary. "It wasn't your fault! There was nothing you could do!" (This is one of the most difficult aspects of SIDS. There is no warning. The baby just stops breathing.)

One more grandparent held her grandbaby for one last time, torn apart with emotion that a normal, healthy baby child had been ripped away from everyone who loved her. How could this be?

The medical examiner, a kind person, said softly, "I know it's hard, Grandma, but we have to go now." The nightmare of loss had begun.

That was three months ago and Grandma Vera is having a hard time. "I hurt so bad! I feel like I have a wound that won't heal. It's pain upon pain to look at Antonia's pictures. Her funeral was held on the same day that our oldest son, Jeff died eighteen years ago. I know the pain my son and daughter-in-law are feeling, and I'm helpless to ease it for them. When I pray, I ask Jesus to help all of us survive this."

Ah, but Jesus is already at work in Vera's life!

Vera has volunteered for more than ten years at a Christian counseling office near her home. Five years ago, she was asked to talk with one of the clients, a SIDS mom, in need of a grandmotherly listener. Vera was reticent, thinking she had little to offer. But the young distraught mom and Vera talked at length by telephone and became good friends. In fact, each year on the anniversary of her friend's loss, Vera sends a card or writes a note of loving care.

Now, five years later and according to the Master's plan, that same SIDS mom is the person assigned by the local office of the SIDS Foundation to help Vera and her son and daughter-in-law work through their grief.

How like our Lord to return a kindness with a kindness!

Vera is blessed with a loving family and many friends who call, visit, and share her hurt. Still, she feels like she has a long way to go.

"As a grandmother, I grieve for the loss of my grandchild and her future—the fluffy dresses and patent leather shoes. But I also grieve for our children and their hurt that I can't make go away and also for our two confused little grandsons who miss their sister, "Baby 'Tonia." Some people ask how I'm doing. I say 'fine.' I want to cry, 'I'm not fine!' But I don't. I believe in the Lord Jesus Christ and I know that he is in control of my life. I know he will heal me. I try to focus on being as much support and comfort as I can to my beloved family."[4]

CRACK GRANDBABY

Leroy is two years old. He came into this world kicking, crying, and every muscle in his body shaking without stopping. Leroy is a crack baby, one of thousands born every year in America today addicted to cocaine. Crack babies are about five percent smaller than drug-free babies. Most are preemies and have a high rate of distress during labor. The cocaine causes premature separation of the placenta from the uterine wall resulting in blood loss for mother and baby and further oxygen deprivation for the baby. Their smaller than normal head size can cause permanent damage such as cerebral palsy, mental retardation, dyslexia, and learning defects.

Leroy's mother was so addicted, she rubbed cocaine on her nipples to ease the pain from the newborn's aggressive sucking, ignorant of the further harm she was causing her son. She is still a user, living in the drug culture.

Social workers searched for a home for Leroy. The only person to come forward was his great-grandmother, Annie, age seventy-six.

Annie is old and ailing but, according to Leroy's social worker, since Leroy came to live with her, she has a stronger will to live so she can be there for Leroy. She is doing everything she can to give this child a loving, stable environment.

"I'm all he's got," says this plucky great-grandmom. "I've got to be all right!"

Leroy weighed one-and-a-half pounds at birth. After finally growing strong enough to go "home," he spent the first few months with his mother, in daily danger. She brought him to Annie's where he has lived since. After a long hospital stay and many sleepless nights being held by his great-grandmother, Leroy, now two, has shed the crack cocaine in his system. What remains are the physical and psychological ramifications, most of which will yet be determined.

How does a seventy-six-year-old great-grandmother manage to care for an active two-year-old—especially one prone to crying fits at the slightest frustration, slow to learn and with a short attention span?

A volunteer from the local social services agency, Mary, takes Leroy one day a week. The other days of the week, he is in state-supported day care from 9 A.M. to 3:30 P.M., and Mary takes him home on weekends. So Leroy not only has a home base with his great-grandmother Annie, he has loving aid and friendship from his state caseworker and a volunteer who goes the extra mile for one little human life.

If something happens to Annie, Leroy will go into the welfare system, probably into foster care. But, thanks to a local volunteer agency worker, Leroy will always have one friend who will follow him wherever he goes, making certain he is all right and that he gets the care he deserves.

And Annie?

"I have had a strong faith in God all of my life. I've prayed every day of my seventy-six years, and I'm just so thankful to God for Mary and the people in my state social services department. Thanks to them, my Leroy is not lost. He's found! And we're going to make his future as bright as it can be!"

CYSTIC FIBROSIS GRANDBABIES

Glenn's wife of thirty-six years died of cancer. Patty's husband of twenty-five years succumbed to a heart attack. Patty and Glenn were brought together nine years ago, Glenn says "by our heavenly Father," and both looked forward to peaceful retirement years. But their heavenly

Father had other plans. Three years ago, Patty and Glenn became legal guardians and medical caregivers to their two grandchildren, ages six and three, who suffer from cystic fibrosis (CF).

Carolyn and her little brother, Ronnie, are not only victims of CF but of drug-addicted and abusive parents as well. Cystic fibrosis is a chronic, inherited, and, thus far, incurable disorder that affects the respiratory and digestive systems. Carolyn's illness is more severe than Ronnie's since she was exposed to heavy smoking by both parents and their friends for the first three years of her life, a disaster for her already impacted lungs. The six-year-old girl receives nourishment from a baby bottle during the day and through a stomach tube at night.

Ronnie, like his sister, takes round-the-clock medications. Nevertheless, he is an active three-year-old. Glenn says he could use a ball and chain for Ronnie. The house had to be "safety-proofed" to protect the little boy from knives, tools, scissors—even the microwave, which he knows how to operate. Like most CF kids, Ronnie and Carolyn are brilliant, quick learners with a keen sense of perception.

Two other grandchildren, Ronnie's and Carolyn's sisters, live in a foster home.

"We just can't take them, too," sixty-eight-year-old Glenn said sadly. "This is all we can handle. But they visit here often and we have some great times!"

Patty's home all day, tending to the children's needs. Earlier this year, the state approved funds for a qualified caregiver to come into the home thirty hours a week to provide respite care so Patty can go shopping, do housework, or take a nap. The state also pays all of the children's medical bills and the grandparents receive social security of $395.

Grandparenting Redefined

This loving, selfless couple is happy with their lot in life. Patty looks at it this way:

"When we first got Carolyn, the prognosis was that she might live to age eight or nine. Now, with continued care, doctors say she may see her thirtieth birthday and perhaps even have a family of her own! I think we got Ronnie at a good time and he's doing fine so far. That's reward enough for me!"

Glenn is quick to add, "I know in my heart that the Lord put these two children with their sweet spirits on this earth for a special purpose. Carolyn looks through religious books with me and always picks out the Savior's picture. Every Sunday, she wants to go to 'Jesus' house' to worship. The Savior loves little children. So do we. This is not a job. It's a privilege! And Ronnie is making me younger every day!"

Ruth Anderson, a senior clinical social worker at a major children's hospital, says that in past years there has been a bias against grandparents taking guardianship of medically needy grandchildren. Today, however, views at public agencies have shifted toward the idea that loving grandparents can play an important role in the well-being of these children.

It is a sad thing to look back upon one's life and recognize that both time and energy have been foolishly wasted on selfish and empty pursuits. Yet, our miracle-working God is he who can cause a harvest of fruitfulness to spring up, even from the soil of our squandered yesterdays.

Pastor Paul LeBoutillier

14
...
Grandparents in Denial

A young father visited my office one day. As we finished our business, he lingered at the door as though he wanted to share something. With my encouragement, he poured out a terrible story of the recent discovery of satanic abuse of his two children, both under the age of ten. He and his wife had befriended a relative, allowing him to live in the spare room for a year. Apparently, in the middle of the night, several times a week, the man had taken the children to a secret coven where unspeakable acts of satanic ritual abuse were performed on them. The children were sworn to secrecy under threat of death, theirs or their parents.

"What you and your parents must be going through!" I was deeply moved.

He shrugged his shoulders, saying, "You mean the kids' grandparents? Mine have passed on and my wife's? They're no help. They have so much garbage they haven't dealt with in their own lives, they're a negative influence. We can't even take the kids over there. My wife and I are fighting our battles alone, with the Lord's help."

Grandparents in denial of their dysfunctions—dysfunctions never allowed to surface—can do a lot of damage. The grandparents' past mistakes are repeated in current family relationships, in this case, robbing two children and their parents of someone to turn to their sorrow, and changing these grandparents into angry, lonely people consumed with guilt. How is the cycle broken?

RECOGNIZING DENIAL

Counselor Jacqueline McCoy says:

It's hard for some of us to know our areas of denial. We all have denial to some extent and that can be healthy as a self-preservation mechanism. Mostly, though, denial is unhealthy and found in addictive families such as those where there is abuse of alcohol, drugs, eating disorders, physical or sexual abuse, or workaholism. Some people enter into multiple marriages, addicted to a person and not a substance. Denial can be hard to recognize in ourselves because it has become such an ingrained pattern in our lives over the years. The hallmark of addiction is denial.

The Bible says in Exodus that the sins of the fathers are passed on to the children through the third and fourth generation. This happens, not because God doesn't love grandchildren, but because it is a basic principle of human nature. When you sin, your children learn from your sin and their children from theirs, and that sin can be passed on by example until the cycle is broken.[1]

Such behavior requires that we take a long, hard look at unwritten rules that keep our dysfunctions going. Unfinished business, left alone, harms others, manifesting itself in meddling, anger, controlling, and dominating, even going so far as to interfere in and sometimes break up a marriage.

An example is the grandparent who had a child out of wedlock and relinquished the child many years ago, never telling anyone. She married and her child from this marriage had a baby out of wedlock and decided to give the baby up for adoption. This was difficult for the grandparent who had never resolved relinquishing her own child. She became so caught up in the relinquishing of the grandchild that all kinds of problems developed between the grandparent and her daughter. The same scenario is played out when a grandparent's abortion is repeated by a daughter and the intense focus on the lost life causes bitterness and pain.

We're back to the issue of control and insecurity. Denial of unhealthy behavior and unfinished business from the past is a complete distortion of reality because of the life we have in Christ. Our needs are not met in a substance, in a thing, or in another person, but by Christ alone. If we look to anyone or anything else, we open ourselves to disappointment and can cause others a world of hurt. The only way to handle denial is to see it for what it is.

GOD IS IN CONTROL

Jesus Christ is life! He is security. He is love. He is everything he has said that he is to us through his Word and by his grace. "Do you not know? Have you not heard? The Lord is the everlasting God, the Creator of the ends of the earth. He will not grow tired and weary, and his understanding no one can fathom. He gives strength to the weary and increases the power of the weak. Even youths grow tired and weary, and young men stumble and fall; but those who hope in the Lord will renew their strength. They will soar on wings like eagles; they will run and not grow weary, they will walk and not be faint" (Isa. 40:28-31).

THE ROAD TO RENEWAL

There can be many reasons why young parents don't bring the kids over to see Grandma and Grandpa and why grandchildren don't want to come:

- Grandpa drinks too much
- Grandpa hits Grandma
- Grandpa swears
- Grandma is too critical
- Grandma buys expensive presents I can't afford
- Grandpa touches me in my private places
- Grandma and Grandpa are never happy

Issues like these, and many more, usually have something or everything to do with denial of some unfinished, unrecognized business—bitterness, unforgiven hurts, anger—from Grandma and/or Grandpa's past. They almost always have to do with "control," where the grandparent can see only one point of view of a given situation, a view tainted with murky memories that shut out the reality of what is good and enriching for the young parent or grandchild. Or past memories are so bound up in a secret place that no one ever sees them except when they show up in bombastic, lecherous, or otherwise destructive ways.

The road to renewal begins when we see ourselves as others see us, when we take that first step out of dark denial to allow investigation of the burdens that hold us hostage from loving, caring relationships today. It's tough to handle burdens like abuse, anger, distrust, unfulfilled expectations, and sins of the past alone. Locating a reputable Christian counselor is an essential next step. Walking through the pain of the past isn't easy, but once the road-blocks begin to clear away and the path to wholeness is in sight, we can be on our way to grandparenting as God intended it to be.

From her years of experience as a Christian counselor, Lorraine Picker offers this prescription for grandparents in denial:

"It's never too late to deal with it, to trace it back and find out how the pattern started. Where did this dysfunction come from? How did the enemy get into this family and what is the source of any anger and bitterness? There is almost always a parent involved, usually the father. Once we expose the source, we can concentrate on breaking the stronghold. How?

1. *Stop blaming.* Own the problem. As long as you are in the blaming department, you will never get out.

2. *Take responsibility.* Step firmly out of the role of the "innocent victim" into responsibility for past, present, and future actions.

3. *Repent earnestly.* Take authority over the generational curse to free yourself of it forever.[2]

REBUILDING TRUST

Once a grandparent has stepped out of denial into new life the process of rebuilding the trust of loved ones takes time. Picker advises, "Ask the Lord for the ability to communicate that there has been a change. God has done something in your life. Begin with the parents of your grandchildren. When parents realize the joyous difference, they can be valuable allies in rebuilding the trust of a beloved grandchild. Parents can say to their children, 'Jesus does change people and we pray for Grandpa (or Grandma.) Look what he is doing in Grandpa's life! See how happy he is today! See how much he loves you!'

173

Grandparenting Redefined

Children will also notice the change and will be drawn to you."[3]

I can't imagine a grandparent who wouldn't want to try. Where there is honest repentence, the blood of Jesus cleanses the sin.

Ever since Eve, Abels and Cains have been stepping on parents' and grandparents' hearts. Blinded by pain, we often overlook the step needed to restore broken relationships and free ourselves to love unconditionally once more. That step? Forgiveness. To forgive is to release, set at liberty, to acquit.

We must do it. The Lord requires it of us.

Quin Sherrer

15
...

Forgiving Grandparents

When we forgive someone who has disappointed or hurt us, we clear the debris from cracked relationships, making way for the Holy Spirit to minister wholeness in our lives.

C.S. Lewis said, "God sometimes speaks to us most intimately when He catches us off our guard."[1] We know deep down in our hearts if we have areas of unforgiveness. During an off-guard moment we may find ourselves longing to hear the voice of an estranged loved one. We may ache for the touch of a distant child, a child who never comes. We yearn for restoration of happy family times, or when that is not possible, we need to bring closure to what has happened. By holding back forgiveness, we make the cracks in the relationship longer, wider, and harder for God to mend.

Grandparents find it necessary to extend forgiveness to

adult children or grandchildren for any number of reasons: ingratitude, lying, rejection, stealing, harsh words, and harsher actions. You might be thinking, *I've been so hurt! They should do the apologizing! They are the ones who should ask me for forgiveness!*

True as that may be, it may never happen. For the sake of your own peace of mind and heart, you may need to reach out to them.

I warn you, though. Watch out for miracles! When you mix love and forgiveness, expect an explosion of grace. And God's grace is greater than the deepest hurt. God can turn your simple, straightforward words of forgiveness toward another into new life for the person in need of your forgiveness. As he releases you from your burden, he can empower your words to cut like a sword through a stone— the stone heart of the guilty one.

Ever see flowers growing from a stone? Mighty God can make it happen! Someone has to start the process. Is that someone you?

To forgive another is a conscious choice. When we choose to forgive, no matter how hard it is, we extend the love and mercy Paul wrote about in Ephesians 4:32: "Be kind and compassionate to one another, forgiving each other, just as in Christ God forgave you."

Then you can let the Holy Spirit take it from there.

Do it quickly. There's no time like the present! Before it festers or festers any longer. If you can, go to the person. Keep it simple. There's no need for fancy phrases.

"I know you felt badly about what happened yesterday, and I want you to know I forgive you for what you did. I love you."

"I know you've been under a lot of pressure lately, and I want you to know I forgive you for not keeping in touch. I'm praying for you and looking forward to the time you can come for a long visit. I love you."

In her book, *How To Forgive Your Children*, Quin Sherrer says, "Forgiving, by God's plan, is to freely bestow favor on the one who has offended us. Jesus clearly instructed us to: 'Forgive, and you will be forgiven' (Luke 6:37). Here forgive means to 'let loose from,' or 'to release, set at liberty.' When we forgive, we free both ourselves and the one forgiven; our choice gives God the freedom to release both of us."[2]

CLEARING THE AIR

Lois and her daughter, Jenny, are good friends and spend a lot of time together accompanied by the grand-children, Matt, nine, and Marcie, two. Over the years, many of Jenny's mothering methods bothered Lois, but she didn't feel she could speak up. After all, they were small things.

One day, the four of them were at the mall. Matt wanted to see a favorite movie so everybody went. But the baby was fussy, and, as usual, when the baby fussed, Grandma took care of her. Marcie cried through the movie so Grandma Lois walked with her out in the theater lobby. Matt munched on popcorn and anything else he asked for.

After the movie, Marcie hadn't let up. Always an irri-table child, today was a *bad* day! And Grandma was wearing out. But young Matt was raring to go and cajoled his mother into taking him to the video arcade in the mall. Grandma endured another hour with her increasingly un-happy granddaughter while Jenny allowed Matt to do anything he wanted.

Grandma's angry thoughts began to creep in. *She always favors Matt! Doesn't she realize that Marcie needs to be home? Can't she see the burden this is placing on me?*

At long last, Matt ran out of quarters and as everyone

got into the car to go home, Grandma was sullen and obviously upset.

"What's the matter, Grandma?" asked Matt, happily.

Lois couldn't resist the question.

"Well, Matt, I'll tell you! You saw your movie, and your little sister cried all the way through it. Then your mom took you to play video games, and you heard Marcie screaming. You could have had some consideration for your sister and for me and not been so selfish!"

Mother heard all of this from the backseat. The ride home was silent except for Marcie's uncontrollable crying.

By the time the group arrived home, both mother and grandmother were in tears, and the anger poured out as soon as Marcie had been bedded down.

"How dare you talk to Matt like that!"

"Look, Jenny, I know you waited six years to have Matt. I know how special he is to you, but you don't realize how you favor him at Marcie's expense. This whole uncomfortable afternoon could have been avoided with a little discipline from you!"

Jenny was furious, walked off, and slammed the bedroom door. Grandma gathered her purse to leave as Matt bolted through the front door and threw his arms around his grandma.

"I love you, Grandma. I'm sorry if I hurt your feelings and when Marcie wakes up, I'll say I'm sorry to her, too, okay?" Jenny peered with teary eyes through the half-open bedroom door at Grandma. In a moment of time, their hearts melted and, as Matt threw his coat over a chair and dashed for the refrigerator, mother and daughter embraced.

"Forgive me, Sweetheart. It's just that I've watched you overindulge Matt so many times and been silent. I guess it all came pouring out at once. In most ways you are doing a *super* job of raising the children. I made so many mistakes as a parent. The Lord knows I'm not perfect! Please forgive me?"

"It's okay, Mom. You're right. I *do* favor Matt. We just waited so long for him, I got caught up in spoiling him. But I have to stop. Thanks for showing me that I'm not helping Matt *or* Marcie! I love you, Mom. Will you forgive me?"

What happened here? Matt's behavior triggered unresolved anger, and mother and grandmother experienced the backlash of their own stored-up guilt and preconceived ideas. Willingness to clear the air led to refreshing candor between both women, even about burdens from childhood that Jenny had carried for thirty years.

If the person is far away or has died, there is still a way to accomplish forgiveness. The way is, of course, by speaking forgiveness to our heavenly Father. Lay the burden at his feet. He will assume your hurt and release your debt.

If you grew up with Philippians 4:8, you know it does *not* say, "Whatever is bitter, whatever is angry, whatever is resentful . . . think about such things."

No. It says, "Whatever is true, whatever is noble, whatever is right, whatever is pure, whatever is lovely, whatever is admirable—if anything is excellent or praiseworthy—think about such things."

Ask yourself, "Have I dwelled on such things or have I allowed the log in my eye to distort and obstruct what God would have me see? Have I seen the truth and not spoken up out of fear of rejection? Have I replaced praise and admiration with bitterness and resentment? Am I the one to begin the healing process by freely extending forgiveness in the name of Jesus?"

C.S. Lewis also said, "Beware of permanent emotions."[3] Never say never! If you keep the door ajar, Christ will come in.

A GRANDPARENT'S PRAYER OF FORGIVENESS

We know that much of our difficulty in forgiving comes from the circumstances of divorce when it invades our lives and our kids' lives. Counselor Lorraine Picker offers this prayer for grandparents in need of healing:

> Heavenly Father, in the name of Jesus, we forgive our son and daughter-in-law for not teaching our grandchildren the values we taught them. We forgive them for divorcing and failing to provide a home where our grandchildren might have their needs for love and security met. We forgive them for the pain and heartache they have caused us. We pray for repentance and reconciliation. We thank you, Lord, for healing our hearts.[4]

Who wins?

Your loved one does. God does. You do! Forgiveness is sweetness like a beam of God's glory. It is a holy thing.

"The plea of God is to *keep* handing down the true truth—don't miss a generation. He wants people to *know*; it is to continue to be known. In Psalms 81:13, 16 we have the compassionate words of God which remind us of Jesus weeping over Jerusalem because the people turned away: 'Oh, that my people had hearkened unto me, and Israel had walked in my ways . . . He should have fed them also with the finest of the wheat: and with honey out of the rock should I have satisfied thee" (KJV).

God's direct word comes to us—consider your place in the family as central . . . Don't let a gap come because of you. Don't take the beauty of the family life—and the reality of being able to hand down true truth to one more generation—as a light thing. It is one of the central commands of God." [1]

Edith Schaeffer

16
...
A Grandparent's Legacy

When I was a little girl my Grandma Burch told me that every time you think kindly about someone who has died, God bestows a blessing on that person in heaven. So when our dog, King, got lost and didn't return, I thought about him often so God would bless him in a big way.

As I grew older, loss impacted my life in a more serious and indelible way.

I was fifteen years old when Grandma Burch went to heaven. The yellowed newspaper story says fourteen of her seventeen children and many of her 121 direct descendants attended the funeral service in Deer Lodge, Montana.

I had not known my grandma for all of the years of togetherness that my friend, Caralee, knew hers. Our large and growing family moved to Oregon before my teen years. We had only spent very little time with Grandma and Grandpa. But the time we shared made a lasting, perhaps eternal, impression on me. Grandma Burch, especially, left me a legacy of love, strength, wisdom, courage, and faith.

She died in 1949. I figure by now she's about the best blessed grandma in heaven!

And my beloved mother lives beside her. I have no doubt that her twenty-eight grandchildren and seven great-grandchildren are raising her heavenly blessing count daily.

HEROES

The Persian Gulf War rekindled the fire of patriotism in America. The men and women of the armed forces came home heroes. And do we need more heroes!

Grandpa, are you a hero to your grandchildren? In these changing times, a grandfather can step in to fill the void of a father figure in a grandchild's life.

Colleen Townsend Evans was greatly impacted by her grandfather as she shares in this intimate story:

I grew up poor and fatherless. Not ideal—yes, I know. But I consider that I had a privileged childhood. Let me explain . . .

Divorced shortly after I was born, my mother moved the two of us into her widowed father's simple home. My grandfather, an immigrant, was an idealistic man of great strength of character. A person of few words, he nevertheless had the capacity to communicate unconditional love and acceptance to the little girl who had invaded his world. (If he resented that invasion, I never knew.)

In the years that followed, I had the joy of growing up with a hero! That's what my grandfather was to me. And I earnestly pray that God will enable me to make each of our incredible grandchildren feel as uniquely special and unconditionally loved as my grandfather did for me.[2]

Gloria Gaither writes this about heroes:

The little fellow was playing on the floor with his trucks that fine spring morning. His grandma was standing at the sink washing a dishpanful of tender fresh leaf lettuce, some of the first to be harvested in town.

What are you going to be when you grow up? the grandmother asked the child.

The boy crawled across the floor pushing his toy tractor, making motor noises with his mouth.

Would you like working in a big factory or having an office of your own? Are you going to be a teacher or maybe a fireman or policeman?

The child crawled closer to the back screen door open to the pungent fragrance of freshly turned soil. He ran his tractor up the door, then stopped, looking out at his grandfather, plowing the warm earth with his garden tractor.

Nope, he finally said, I just wanna be a man. Like my grandpa!

Lord,
Our world is so in need of heroes.
Give us fewer 'professionals'
and more men who stand tall
in integrity and gentle strength and godliness.
Thank you that a real one lives at our house.
Amen.[3]

TWO WORDS TO LEAVE BEHIND

The question we can now ask ourselves is this: "In these changing times, in a world where innocent children risk falling prey to so much evil, what legacy are we leaving our grandchildren? Is it temporary or is it eternal?"

One cold Montana morning, while I sat drinking the forbidden coffee with heaps of fresh cream and sugar, my grandma said, "Don't listen to me. No one alive can ever take the place of the Master Teacher. Study him."

Study him! In those two words are a philosophy of life each of us can pass on to our grandchildren.

Study His Strength

God says his strength is sufficient for us. Scripture teaches our grandchildren that we can do *some* things, not *all* things. Only God can do *all* things. There's such freedom in acknowledging God's strength. It frees us to give the difficult things about which we can do nothing to him.

• "The Lord is my strength and my song; he has become my salvation" (Ex. 15:2).

• "It is God who arms me with strength and makes my way perfect" (2 Sam. 22:33).

• "Look to the Lord and his strength; seek his face always" (1 Chron.16:11).

• "Do not grieve, for the joy of the Lord is your strength" (Neh. 8:10).

• "The Lord is my light and my salvation—whom shall I fear? The Lord is the stronghold of my life—of whom shall I be afraid?" (Ps. 27:1).

• "My flesh and my heart may fail, but God is the strength of my heart and my portion forever" (Ps. 73:26).

• "I can do everything through him who gives me strength" (Phil. 4:13).

Study His Wisdom

Teach your grandchildren to cope in these changing times by modeling Christ's teachings from the Word. We can leave no greater legacy to our grandchildren than to teach them to lean on the wisdom contained in the Holy Bible.

• "And he said to man, 'The fear of the Lord—that is wisdom, and to shun evil is understanding'" (Job 28:28).

• "For the Lord gives wisdom, and from his mouth come knowledge and understanding" (Prov. 2:6).

• "By wisdom the Lord laid the earth's foundations, by understanding he set the heavens in place" (Prov. 3:19).

• "But God made the earth by his power; he founded the world by his wisdom and stretched out the heavens by his understanding" (Jer. 10:12).

• "If any of you lacks wisdom, he should ask God, who gives generously to all without finding fault, and it will be given to him" (James 1:5).

Study His Truth

Edith Schaeffer reminds us that grandparents are central to the family unit. God has entrusted us to hand down the truth and there's only one place to find it. "Thy Word is Truth."

• "I, the Lord, speak the truth. I declare what is right" (Isa. 45:19b).

• "Send forth your light and your truth, let them guide me; let them bring me to your holy mountain, to the place where you dwell" (Ps. 43:3).

• "The Word became flesh and made his dwelling among us. We have seen his glory, the glory of the One and Only, who came from the Father, full of grace and truth" (John 1:14).

• "For the law was given through Moses; grace and truth came through Jesus Christ" (John 1:17).

• "If you hold to my teaching, you are really my disciples. Then you will know the truth, and the truth shall set you free" (John 8:31, 32).

HAVE FUN

Ruth B. Graham told us so beautifully at the beginning of this book about the fun her parents had with the Graham children. They were wonderful examples of finding joy and living it for the children to see and share. Wrap your lessons in happy times for a lasting impression.

And be a grandparent on fire for the Lord. A red coal taken from the fire becomes a dead coal.

You've heard it said that our children are our only possessions we can take to heaven. We need to ask ourselves, then, what example we leaving for them to find their way. Are we passing on truth and doing it with a consistent and contagious zeal? Some of our happiest grandparenting times come when we are truly on fire for the Lord and the children see it, feel it, and want to emulate it!

"I am the way, and the truth and the life. No one comes to the Father except by me" (John 14:6). Show them the way—with gusto and without apology.

KEEP ON KEEPIN' ON

Are you a grandparent blessed with good health, happiness, and an unblemished grandparenting season?
Thank God for his many blessings and reach out to the one whose heart is breaking in these changing times.

Are you a grandparent raising your grandchild?
Take that child in your arms and thank God for the privilege.

Are you a grandparent who has lost a precious grandchild to accident, illness, or abuse?
Give that child into Jesus' loving arms for safekeeping. Release. Let go.

190

Are you a brand new grandparent or a soon-to-be grandparent who wants to be the best you can be?

Study him.

Keep praising the Lord with all your heart, soul, and mind. For no matter what is happening in your grandparenting season, God is with you. Place your trust in him.

Source Notes

INTRODUCTION

1. U.S. Department of Commerce, "Population Reports: Marital Status and Living Arrangements" (Washington, D.C.: U.S. Department of Commerce, 1990), Series P-20, No. 450, March 1990, p. 4.

2. Michele Daly, "Second Time Around Parents" 1990 Fact Sheet (Media, PA: Family and Community Service of Delaware County, 1990), p. 1.

3. Michele Daly, "Second Time Around Parents" 1990 Fact Sheet, p. 1.

CHAPTER ONE

1. Erma Bombeck, "Grandparents Are Visible Species," *Seattle Post Intelligencer,* 15 October 1989, p. J5.

CHAPTER TWO

1. Florence Turnidge, personal interview, Seattle, WA, June 1990.

2. Edith Schaeffer, *What Is A Family?* (Old Tappan, NJ: Fleming H. Revell Co., 1975), p. 22.

3. Paul LeBoutillier, personal interview, Ontario, OR, January 1990.

CHAPTER THREE

1. Caralee Hudson, personal interview, Mountlake Terrace, WA, November 1990.

2. U.S. Department of Commerce, "Changes In American Family Life" Current Population Report (Washington, D.C.: U.S. Department of Commerce, 1989), Series P-23, No. 163, August 1989, p. 7.

3. National Committee For the Prevention of Child Abuse, "Current Trends in Child Abuse and Fatalities" (Chicago, IL: National Committee For the Prevention of Child Abuse, 1991), April 1991, p. 3.

4. Michele Daly, personal interview, Media, PA, April 1991.

CHAPTER FOUR

1. Dr. Martin Luther King, speech given on 3 April 1968 in Birmingham, AL, as quoted in *Familiar Quotations*, edited by Emily Morrison Beck (Boston, MA: Little, Brown & Company, 1980), p. 909.

2. Lee Loevinger, as quoted in *The Courage To Grow Old*, Philip L. Berman, editor (New York: Ballantine, 1989), p. 142.

CHAPTER FIVE

1. Judith S. Wallerstein and Jean Berlin Kelly study, as quoted in *What to Do When Your Son or Daughter Divorces* by Dorothy Weiss Gottlieb, Inez Bellow Gottlieb, and Marjorie A. Slavin (New York: Bantam Books, 1988), p. 119, 120.

2. Laurene Johnson and Georglyn Rosenfeld, *Divorced Kids, What you need to know to help kids survive a divorce* (Nashville, TN: Thomas Nelson, 1990), p. 173, 174.

CHAPTER SIX

1. Michelle Cresse, *Jigsaw Families, Solving the Puzzle of Remarriage* (Lynnwood, WA: Aglow Publications, 1989), p. 15.

CHAPTER SEVEN

1. Sylvie deToledo, "Grandparents As Parents, Grandchildren As Children" report (Long Beach, CA: Psychiatric Clinic For Youth, 1990), p. 4.

2. Sylvie deToledo, "Grandparents As Parents, Grandchildren As Children" report, p. 2.

3. Sylvie deToledo, "Grandparents As Parents, Grandchildren As Children" report, p. 2.

4. U.S. Department of Commerce, "Population Reports: Marital Status and Living Arrangements" (Washington, D.C.: U.S. Department of Commerce, 1990), Series P-20, No. 450, March 1990, p. 9.

5. Sylvie deToledo, "Grandparents As Parents, Grandchildren As Children" report , p. 2.

6. Michele Daly, "Second Time Around Parents" 1990 Fact Sheet, p. 1.

7. Sylvie deToledo, personal interview, Long Beach, CA, December 1990.

8. Diane Werner, personal interview, Media, PA, February 1991.

9. Albert and Mary Etta Johnson, personal interview, Anaheim, CA, November 1990.

10. Candy Johnson, personal interview, Long Beach, CA, February 1991.

11. Melody Hudgins, personal interview, Long Beach, CA, February 1991.

12. "I Am A Promise," words by William J. Gaither and Gloria Gaither (Alexandria, IN: Gaither Music Company, 1975). Copyright 1975 by William J. Gaither. All rights reserved. Used by permission.

CHAPTER EIGHT

1. Tina Scher, personal interview, Seattle, WA, March 1991.

2. Michael W. Bugni, personal interview, Seattle, WA, March 1991.

3. Michael W. Bugni, personal interview.

4. Stephanie Edelstein, "Do Grandparents Have Rights?" *Modern Maturity*, December 1990/January 1991, p. 40.

5. Don J. Gough, personal interview, Lynnwood, WA, March 1991.

CHAPTER NINE

1. Jean Lush, personal interviews, Edmonds, WA, June 1990 and March 1991.

2. Jean Lush, personal interviews.

CHAPTER TEN

1. Jacqueline McCoy, personal interview, Seattle, WA, April 1991.

2. Jacqueline McCoy, personal interview.

CHAPTER ELEVEN

1. Karen Cooksey, "Love Takes More Than Words," *Modern Maturity*, December 1990/January 1991, p. 41.

2. Seattle-King County Advisory Council on Aging, "Grandfather Finds Homespun Stories Bridge Distance," *The Seattle Times*, 18 June 1989, p. K3.

3. Lillian Iverson, personal interview, Seattle, WA, April 1990.

4. Karen Cooksey, "Love Takes More Than Words," p. 41.

5. Karen Cooksey, "Love Takes More Than Words," p. 41.

6. Karen Cooksey, "Love Takes More Than Words," p. 41.

CHAPTER TWELVE

1. Larry Burkett, *Using Your Money Wisely* revised edition (Chicago, IL: Moody Press, 1986). p. 77.

2. David Bragonier, personal interview, Bellevue, WA, February 1991.

3. David Bragonier, personal interview.

4. Lyle K. Wilson, personal interview, Mill Creek, WA, March 1991.

5. American Association of Retired Persons, "A Profile of Older Americans" report (Washington, D.C.: American Association of Retired Persons, 1990), December 1990, p. 3.

6. Lyle K. Wilson, personal interview.

CHAPTER THIRTEEN

1. Mickey Cartwright, personal interviews, Seattle, WA, March 1991 and October 1991.

2. Janet Trinkaus, personal interview, Seattle, WA, February 1991.

3. Janet Trinkhaus, personal interview.

4. Vera Fuhrman, personal interviews, Seattle, WA, March 1991 and October 1991.

CHAPTER FOURTEEN

1. Jacqueline McCoy, personal interview, Seattle, WA, April 1991.

2. Lorraine Picker, personal interview, Seattle, WA, March 1991.

3. Lorraine Picker, personal interview.

CHAPTER FIFTEEN

1. C.S. Lewis, *Letters To Malcolm: Chiefly on Prayer* (New York: Harcourt, Brace & World, Inc., 1964), p. 116.

2. Quin Sherrer with Ruthanne Garlock, *How To Forgive Your Children* (Lynnwood, WA: Aglow Publications, 1989), p. 17.

3. C.S. Lewis, *Letters To Malcolm: Chiefly on Prayer,* p. 98.

4. Lorraine Picker, written for *Grandparenting Redefined, Guidance for Today's Family* (Lynnwood, WA: Aglow Publications, 1992), p. 182.

CHAPTER SIXTEEN

1. Edith Schaeffer, *What Is A Family?* p. 132.

2. Colleen Townsend Evans, written for *Grandparenting Redefined, Guidance for Today's Family* (Lynnwood, WA: Aglow Publications, 1992), p. 186.

3. Gloria Gaither, written for *Grandparenting Redefined, Guidance for Today's Family* (Lynnwood, WA: Aglow Publications, 1992), p. 187.

Resources for Grandparents

American Association of Retired Persons (AARP)
1909 K Street NW
Washington, DC 20049
1-800-424-2277

American Self-Help Clearinghouse
St. Clares-Riverside Medical Center
Denville, NJ 07834
(201) 625-7101

Assessment Treatment and Service Center
Thomas W. Shaw, Ph.D.
1981 Orchard Drive
Santa Ana, CA 92707
(714) 756-0093

Grandparenting Redefined

Attorneys at Law

John R. Blackburn
1110 North 175th Street Suite 109
Seattle, WA 98133
(206) 362-2306

Michael W. Bugni
11320 Roosevelt Way NE
Seattle, WA 98125
(206) 365-5500

Don J. Gough
4324 192nd Street SW
Lynnwood, WA 98036
(206) 775-2141

Lyle K. Wilson
Pioneer Bank Building
910 164th Street SE
Mill Creek, WA 98012
(206) 742-9100

Barnabas, Inc.
David Bragonier, Director
3055 112th Avenue NE Suite 111
Bellevue, WA 98004
(206) 643-7524

Bensonhurst Guidance Center
Debra Langosch, ACSW
8620 18th Avenue
Brooklyn, NY 11214
(718) 256-8600

Shirley Borkovec
8256 East Arabian Trail #241
Scottsdale, AZ 85258
(602) 991-3374

Catholic Guardian Society
Red Hook Prevention Program
Molly F. McDougald
732 Henry Street
Brooklyn, NY 11231
(718) 858-8387

Sherry Checkley
2328 SW Dolph Court
Portland, OR 97219
(503) 246-5324

Val Cook
3044 South 2300 East
Salt Lake City, UT 84109
(801) 487-2167

CRISTA Counseling Service
Jacqueline McCoy, Counselor
19303 Fremont Avenue North
Seattle, WA 98133
(206) 546-7215

Cystic Fibrosis Foundation
6931 Arlington Road
Bethesda, MD 20814
(301) 951-4422
1-800-FIGHT CF

Grandparenting Redefined

Desert Hills Grandparent Support Group
Margery J. McFerron
2797 North Introspect Drive
Tucson, AZ 85745
(602) 622-5437

Harold Dunkerson
199-05 112th Avenue
Holis, NY 11412

Enriched Living Workshops
Verna Birkey
P.O. Box 3039
Kent, WA 98032
(206) 859-6362

Family Dynamics, Inc.
Fran Burg
154 Christopher Street
New York, NY 10014

Foundation For Grandparenting
P.O. Box 31
Lake Placid, NY 12946

From Generation To Generation
Sinai Samaritan Medical Center
2000 West Kilbourn
Milwaukee, WI 53233
(414) 937-5999

Grand Survivors
Charles and Barbara Smith
3331 West 600 Street
Jonesboro, IN 46938
(317) 674-8934

Grand-Parents Again
Nancy Eastman, M.S.W.
The Mental Health Center of Greater Manchester
401 Cypress Street
Manchester, NH 03103
(603) 668-4111

Grandparents Against Immorality And Neglect (GAIN)
Laura D. Poole
2106 Venus Drive
Bossier City, LA 71112

Grandparents As Parents (GAP)

Sylvie deToledo
1150 E. 4th St.
Long Beach, CA 90802
(310) 983-6555

c/o Family Service Association of San Antonio
3203 Nacagdoches Road Suite 200
San Antonio, TX 78217
(512) 657-4748

Grandparenting Redefined

Judy Kingston
5 Greenwood Avenue
Pembroke, MA 02359
(617) 293-5065

Peggy Plante
3235 Farrington Street
Quincy, MA 02170

Lois Schneider
1680 Flicker Lane
Paradise, CA 95969
(916) 877-0118

Mamie Weddington
12134 Kenn Road
Cincinnati, OH 45240

c/o Women's Life at St. Luke's
103 West State Street
Boise, ID 83702
(208) 386-3033

Grandparents as Substitute Parents (GASP)
Pat DenHouten
1099 Brookside Drive
Grand Ledge, MI 48834
(517) 627-4138

Grandparents In Touch
Luetta G. Werner, M.S.
5831 Kipling Ct.
Lincoln, NE 68516

Grandparents Offering Love and Direction (GOLD)
700 North Johnson Suite O
El Cajon, CA 92020
(619) 447-7349

Grandparents Raising Grandchildren

Barbara Kirkland
P.O. Box 104
Colleyville, TX 76034

Maury Lambert, ACSW, BCD
Dept. of Social Work and Discharge Planning
Providence Hospital
Everett, WA 98206
(206) 258-7577

George and Tina Scher
20227 87th Avenue West
Edmonds, WA 98026
(206) 774-9721

Mignon Scherer, Ph.D Cd.
3851 Centraloma Drive
San Diego, CA 92107
(619) 223-0344

Grandparents Support Group of Los Angeles
Tiney Harris
1887 Cordova #4
Los Angeles, CA 90007
(213) 733-9312

Grandparenting Redefined

Grandparents Support Group - Thrift Store
Ruby E. Miller
1140 Almond Tree Lane Suite 311
Las Vegas, NV 89104
(702) 732-4668

Grandparents Who Care
Sue Trupin, R.N., Co-Director
P.O. Box 24576
San Francisco, CA 94124
(415) 822-4457

Grandparents'—Children's Rights
Ann Conkright
424 East Stanford
Springfield, MO 65807
(417) 862-9862
(Groups also established in Joplin, Kansas City, Kirksville,
St. Louis, and Hermitage.)

Iverson Center
Lorraine Picker, Counselor
424 North 130th Street
Seattle, WA 98133
(206) 367-4600

Ralph and Mary Jerger
4265 South 700 East
Marion, IN 46953

Esther Kershaw
9040 South 400 West
Fairmount, IN 46928
(317) 948-4466

Madeleine Labore
P.O. Box 79
Suncook, NH 03275-0079
(603) 485-7341

LOVE, Unconditional
Linda J. Friedrich
1053 Cloverdale Drive
Mobile, AL 36606
(205) 653-1174

Bob and Shirley Maxey
313 Mockingbird South
Altus, OK 73521
(405) 482-3545

Mental Health Association of Broward County
Connie Harrell, Parents Projects Coordinator
5546 West Oakland Park Boulevard Suite 207
Lauderhill, FL 33313
(305) 733-3994

Mental Development Center
Tearalla Lee
11130 Bellflower
Cleveland, OH 44106

Mary Ellen Miller
Route #1 Box 191B
Auburn, PA 17922
(717) 754-7313

Grandparenting Redefined

More Than Grandparents
Elaine Kahaner
Manchester Memorial Hospital
71 Haynes Street
Manchester, CT 06040
(203) 646-1222 extension 2405

Connie L. Mulholland
17458 Mapledale Avenue
Port Charlotte, FL 33953
(813) 629-4065

Navigators
P.O. Box 6000
Colorado Springs, CO 80934

Northwest Family Center
1536 U Street NW 3rd Floor
Washington, DC 20009
(202) 673-2042

Oldies With Little Ones (OWLS)
Sydney Fryberger
510A Ryan Road
Buckley, WA 98321
(206) 829-1634

Ottawa County Community Mental Health Services
Prevention Services
Lorraine Harper, M.S.W.
12265 James Street
Holland, MI 49424-9661
(616) 392-1873

Pierce County Health Department
Edith Owen
3629 South D Street
Tacoma, WA 98408
(206) 591-6490

Positive Directions
Joan M. Stokes, M.S.
777 South State Road 7 Suite 10
Margate, FL 33311
(305) 979-3655

Raising Others' Children
Sandra Campbell and Emma Wilson
1815 South 18th Street
Philadelphia, PA 19145
(215) 271-0053

Raising Our Children's Kids (ROCK)
Jessie Taylor
2501 Leonard Street #202
Duluth, MN 55811
(218) 723-8187

Rise 'N Shine Foundation
1305 Fourth Avenue
Seattle, WA 98101
(206) 628-8949

Mary Louise Robinson
1740 Page Street
San Francisco, CA 94117
(415) 621-3361

Grandparenting Redefined

Santa Maria Community Services, Inc.
Grandparent's Group Coordinator
2104 Saint Michael Street
Cincinnati, OH 45204
(513) 921-4271

Second Time Around Parents (STAP)
Family and Community Services of Delaware County
Michele Daly
100 West Front Street
Media, PA 19063
(217) 566-7540

SIDS Alliance
10500 Little Patuxent Parkway Suite 420
Columbia, MD 21044
1-800-221-SIDS

Joan Steele
1040 Rosedale Road
Venice, FL 34293

OTHER BOOKS BY AGLOW PUBLICATIONS

Heart Issues

Stanley C. Baldwin **If I'm Created in God's Image Why Does It Hurt to Look in the Mirror?**
A True View of You

Janet Bly **Friends Forever**
The Art of Lifetime Relationships

Gloria Chisholm **The Gift of Encouragement**
How to be a Warm Shoulder in a Cold World

Michelle Cresse **Beyond Fear**
The Quantum Leap to Courageous Living

Jigsaw Families
Solving the Puzzle of Remarriage

Heather Harpham **Daddy, Where Were You?**
Healing for the Father-Deprived Daughter

Diana Kruger **Who Says Winners Never Lose?**
Profiting from Life's Painful Detours

Pam Ravan **Sock Hunting and Other Pursuits of the Working Mother**

Patricia H. Rushford **Lost in the Money Maze?**
How to Find Your Way Through

Marie Sontag **When Love Is Not Perfect**
Discover God's Re-parenting
Process

General Books

Barbara Cook **Love and Its Counterfeits**

Marion Duckworth **What's Real Anyway?**
Eternal Living in an Everyday
World

Carol Greenwood **A Rose for Nana**
& Other Touches from an Everyday God

Ranelda Mack
Hunsicker **Secrets**
Unlocking the Mystery of Inti-
macy With God

Kathy Collard
Miller **Healing the Angry Heart**
A Strategy for Confident
Mothering

Sure Footing in a Shaky World
A Woman's Journey to Security

Quin Sherrer **How to Pray for Your Children**

Quin Sherrer with
Ruthanne Garlock **How to Forgive Your Children**

| Joanne Smith and | **How to Say Goodbye** |
| Judy Biggs | Working Through Personal Grief |

We at Aglow Publications want to encourage you to stop into your Christian bookstore and pick up these books. If, however, you do not have access to a Christian bookstore, you may order toll-free at 1-800-755-2456.

Inquiries regarding speaking availability and other correspondences may be directed to Irene Endicott at the following address:

Irene Endicott
P.O. Box 532
Kirkland, WA 98083